Dana,

Please accept this small token of appreciation for all the hardwork you have accomplished during the last year and a half and as a Christmas gift from me to you. It has been a sincere pleasure to work alongside you the last several months and I look forward to the next year and a half we have left. You are a real leader in my book, so continue to strive for bigger & better within this great organization. I know you can.

Sincerely,

Sen Tobriello, LCPL, USCG

Character in Action

CHARACTER in ACTION

The U.S. COAST GUARD on LEADERSHIP

Donald T. Phillips
with Adm. James M. Loy, USCG (Ret.)

Naval Institute Press
Annapolis, Maryland

Naval Institute Press
291 Wood Road
Annapolis, MD 21402

Library of Congress Cataloging-in-Publication Data
Phillips, Donald T. (Donald Thomas), 1952–
    Character in action: the U.S. Coast Guard on leadership /
Donald T. Phillips and James M. Loy.
        p.   cm.
    Includes index.
    ISBN 1-59114-672-0 (alk. paper)
    1. United States. Coast Guard. 2. Leadership. I. Loy, James
M., 1942– II. Title.
    VG53.P49 2003
    658.4'092—dc21
                                                2003008059

Printed in the United States of America on acid-free paper ∞
10 09 08 07 06 05 04 03   9 8 7 6 5 4 3 2
First printing

This book is dedicated to members of the
United States Coast Guard—past, present, and future.
All author royalties are donated to Coast Guard Mutual Assistance.

Contents

Part Four. Ensure the Future

Prologue

We the people of the United States, in order to form a more perfect
union, establish justice, insure domestic tranquility, provide for
the common defense, promote the general welfare, and
secure the blessings of liberty to ourselves and our
posterity, do ordain and establish this
Constitution of the United
States of America.

Preamble to the Constitution of the
United States of America, ratified 21 June 1788

Always keep in mind that [your] countrymen are freemen, and, as such,
are impatient of everything that bears the least mark of a domineering
spirit. . . . Endeavor to overcome difficulties by a cool and
temperate perseverance in [your] duty-by [skill]
and moderation, rather than by
vehemence or violence.

—Alexander Hamilton,
in a letter of advice to members of the newly
created Revenue-Marine, 4 July 1791

With the swearing in of George Washington as the nation's first president on 30 April 1789, the American Revolution finally came to an end. The war had been won, the nation founded. Now it was time to build. As Washington phrased it, "My hope was to gain time for the country to progress without interruption to that degree of strength . . . necessary to give it command of its own fortunes."

Of particular concern for the new president was the establishment of economic stability in the wake of the $70 million debt accumulated during the war. To lead this monumental task, Washington chose Alexander Hamilton—his friend and former aide-de-camp who had fought with him at Trenton, slogged through Valley Forge with the troops, and had been on hand for the surrender at Yorktown. After the fighting, Hamilton had served as a delegate from New York and voted for the new constitution in spite of the fact that the rest of his delegation refused to support it. He then worked with James Madison and John Jay to write the Federalist Papers that promoted ratification.

As the first U.S. secretary of the treasury, Alexander Hamilton created a broad-based economic plan, including a major focus on shipping, which, at the time, was the world's primary mode for commerce and trade. Among other things, he proposed customs duties and tariffs on imported goods, graduated tax rates on revenue, and various shipping dues. He also advocated federal responsibility for ensuring safety at sea for ships and their crews and cargoes.

To make these new initiatives work, Hamilton believed that "a few armed vessels, judiciously stationed at the entrances of our ports might, at a small expense, be made useful sentinels of the laws." Accordingly, he proposed the formation of a "strong right arm" for the new nation—a seagoing military force that would enforce customs and navigation laws, cruise the coasts, hail in-bound ships, make inspections, and certify manifests.

The First United States Congress, in one of its initial pieces of legislation, formally approved Alexander Hamilton's proposal. The act of 4 August 1790 provided for "the establishment and support of ten cutters" along with the creation of a professional corps of forty commissioned officers to man the new service. Hamilton also recommended to Congress that it give the cutter personnel the rank and standing of military officers—because, as he said, "it would attach them to their duty by a nicer sense of honor."

Mindful of why the American Revolution had been fought in the first place, Hamilton then penned a letter of advice to personnel of the newly created Revenue-Marine. "Always keep in mind that [your] countrymen are freemen," he wrote, "and, as such, are impatient of everything that bears the least mark of a domineering spirit. . . . Refrain from haughtiness, rudeness, or insult. . . . Endeavor to overcome difficulties by a cool and temperate perseverance in [your] duty—by [skill] and moderation, rather than by vehemence or violence." He advised that the officers' demeanor and behavior "be marked with prudence, moderation, and good temper. Upon these qualities must depend the success, usefulness and . . . continuance of the establishment in which they are included."

Finally, Alexander Hamilton stated that his words of advice had been "selected with careful attention to character"—and that all personnel "should take the oath to support the Constitution of the United States."

And so the roots of the United States Coast Guard were planted.

Character in Action

Introduction

In the U.S. Coast Guard:
There are no spectators.
There is a hero around every corner.
Safety and *Protection* are the cornerstone watchwords.

Close your eyes and place a finger anywhere on a map of the United States and you're likely to pinpoint a place where the United States Coast Guard is providing some sort of valuable service to the nation. Wherever there are cargo ships, sailboats, motorboats, bridges, ports of entry, or ice fishing—the Coast Guard is there. Wherever there is a problem in navigable U.S. waters with drugs, illegal immigrants, customs, or smuggling, the Coast Guard is there. Whenever and wherever there is a need for homeland security or operations in the defense of the United States, the Coast Guard is on hand performing its duty. It often operates without fanfare, routinely in support of other government agencies, frequently initiating and leading the action. And, of course, every American knows that when they are in trouble at sea, the Coast Guard will answer their distress call, promptly and efficiently.

The United States Coast Guard is one of America's five military services. Although it is known primarily for search and rescues at sea, that mission is just the tip of the iceberg of jobs the organization performs. Seven-eighths of an iceberg lies below the surface, and the Coast Guard has at least twelve other missions formally authorized by the United States Congress. Here's what the U. S. Coast Guard does, twenty-four hours a day, seven days a week, all year, every year.

SEARCH AND RESCUE

The Coast Guard has direct responsibility for search and rescue (SAR) on the high seas and navigable waterways for commercial fisherman, sport fishermen, recreational boaters, cargo ships, cruise ships, and all who go to sea. In Alaska, a typical SAR case could cover a distance equal to that from Seattle to New York. The Coast Guard responds to emergency 911 calls on the water for heart attack victims, injuries, and all those in peril on the sea.

ENVIRONMENTAL RESPONSE

The Coast Guard responds to natural disasters, including hurricanes, tornadoes, flooding, and the like. When everybody else is evacuating, the Coast Guard is coming in and staying. It also responds to man-made disasters, including oil spills, terrorist activity, and plane crashes, and takes action to prevent environmental pollution.

MARITIME LAW ENFORCEMENT

The Coast Guard participates in enforcement of all federal laws on, under, and over all U.S. waters. This includes protection of the United States' 120 international maritime agreements as well as suppression of smuggling, illicit drug traffic, and illegal immigration. It also participates in enforcement and protection of all the nation's fisheries. In the Bering Sea and Gulf of Alaska alone, which is estimated to provide 40–60 percent of the protein biomass in the world, it is a $7–10 billion business. The Coast Guard protects all U.S. fisheries from foreign encroachment, and regulates vessels regarding time, catch quotas, and size and types of fish that may be caught. It also provides enforcement of all marine environmental protection laws, including the Marine Mammal Protection Act and the Endangered Species Act.

AIDS TO NAVIGATION

The Coast Guard has direct responsibility for navigational safety in U.S. waters, including short-range aids to navigation and the design and operation of vessel traffic services. It enforces regulation of voice radio communications for vessels and operates radio aids to navigation, including the LORAN (Long Range Aid to Navigation) System. It has direct responsibility for operation and maintenance of aids to navigation, such as lighthouses, lightships, fog signals, beacons, and buoys. The Coast Guard routinely maintains buoys that weigh as much as 20,000 pounds from the Aleutian Islands of Alaska (where the wind-chill can get as low as 20 degrees below zero) to the sweltering, hundred-degree heat of Louisiana.

MARITIME INSPECTION

The Coast Guard has direct responsibility for vessel safety inspection, including inspection of foreign vessels, to ensure conformance to international law. It also provides enforcement of required equipment regulations for boats and all sea-going vessels, including cruise ships. The Coast Guard enforces regulation of deepwater ports, offshore terminals, deep seabed mining, and ocean thermal energy conversion projects. It also assists in control and designation of anchorages.

MARITIME LICENSING

The Coast Guard has direct responsibility for the examination, licensing, and certification of U.S. merchant mariners, as well as administration of pilotage services on the Great Lakes.

WATERWAYS MANAGEMENT

The Coast Guard has direct responsibility for regulation of bridges over navigable waterways everywhere in the United States. That responsibility extends to the management of 361 commercial ports and includes, for example, all barge traffic going up and down the Mississippi River.

Boating Safety

The Coast Guard has responsibility for the establishment and enforcement of boating safety standards nationwide. It developed and directs a national boating safety program for small craft, including preventative measures to promote safety, and disseminates marine safety information.

Maritime Science

The Coast Guard delivers weather and oceanographic services for numerous other federal agencies throughout the world. It provides logistical and transportation support for scientific missions ranging from the polar ice caps to deep ocean floor dredging for scientific purposes.

Ice Operations

The Coast Guard has direct responsibility for domestic ice breaking for the express purpose of keeping commerce and trade open. Its duties also include ice breaking for scientific research and reconnaissance, iceberg warning service off Newfoundland, and operation of the International Ice Patrol, which charts iceberg movement into shipping lanes.

Port Safety and Security

The Coast Guard has direct responsibility for the safety and security of all shipping ports and marine ports of entry into the United States, such as New York Harbor, Houston Ship Channel, and ports from Puerto Rico to Alaska, from Guam to Maine.

Homeland Security

The Coast Guard has direct responsibility for all issues dealing with the

security of American citizens along the nation's coasts and inland waterways, including regulation of maritime approaches and the carriage of hazardous materials.

DEFENSE OPERATIONS

As a military service, the Coast Guard has a responsibility for national
defense of the United States. It has served in every major war in which the
country has been involved. This service has included convoy escorts, coastal
and offshore patrols, port safety operations, operation of transports and
invasion craft, participation in antisubmarine and amphibious landing
operations, and interaction with foreign navies.

With all of these formal missions, the Coast Guard's foundation continues
to be its fundamentally humanitarian mission. It is bound to a heritage of
service to the public that is routinely credited with saving more than three
thousand lives each year. After the Revenue-Marine was formed in 1790, additional marine public service organizations were created, such as the Lighthouse
Service, the Lifesaving Service, and the Steamboat Inspection Service, to name
a few. On 28 January 1915, these were merged into one organization to form
the modern-day Coast Guard. It has been known by such monikers as
"Guardians of the Sea," "Smokies of the Sea," "The Law on the Sea," and
"The Lifesavers." And throughout its history, "safety" and "protection" have
been the Coast Guard's cornerstone watchwords.

Over the years, the American people have come to count on the Coast
Guard to keep them safe on the water, to keep the water itself safe from environmental disaster, and to maintain the safety and efficiency of commerce
upon which the nation's economic health depends. Remarkably, however,
most citizens do not realize that the Coast Guard is a relatively small organization, that it is usually understaffed, and that, every day, it routinely does
more with less than any other group in the U.S. government.

While the Coast Guard has more than two hundred stations around the
nation, it has only 38,000 active members—a smaller number than the New
York City Police Department and only a fraction (less than 3 percent) of the
active forces in the rest of the U.S. military (1.37 million). Moreover, the

Coast Guard gets the job done on an annual shoestring budget of less than 2 percent of the combined multibillion-dollar budget of the other four military services—less than the cost of one new aircraft carrier.

The inevitable question, of course, is: "How does the Coast Guard do so much, so efficiently, with so few people, and so little money?"

The answer falls into two parts.

First, it's the people. There are no spectators in the Coast Guard. Everybody performs several jobs. It is an organization filled with inspired, dedicated people of character and humility who, as it happens, do great things every day. In a very literal sense, there is a hero around every corner. And, what's more, every single member knows the Coast Guard missions and their own role in those missions.

Second, the United States Coast Guard lives and breathes leadership. It pervades every aspect of an organization where every person is a leader.

Most studies of leadership involve a single person—one leader who has made a difference in an organization. But this is the story of an organization that has made a difference in the success of a nation. The roots of the Coast Guard go back to the birth of the United States of America. It was a service organization imbued with proper leadership thinking and behavior by the nation's founders. That leadership has endured for more than two and one-quarter centuries, uncorrupted by the "business management" thinking of the industrial age, tested by war, and tempered by terrorism in the homeland.

So read on, now, and see how the United States Coast Guard, as an organization, has become the living embodiment of great leadership—and how, every day, its people personify character in action.

PART ONE Set the Foundation

Chapter 1

Define the Culture and
Live the Values

We in the Coast Guard go with a good group of people out to a place where
only our training, our maintenance, and our relationships with each
other combine to help ensure our survival. Because the Coast
Guard is inextricably intertwined with the sea, we are at
one with nature—but only if we work together.

—Coast Guard captain

Semper Paratus (Always Ready)

—Official motto, U.S. Coast Guard

Honor, Respect, Devotion to Duty

—Core Values, U.S. Coast Guard

In March 2000, the Master Chief Petty Officer of the Coast Guard received a
letter from a retired enlisted man who told of an incident that had happened
twenty years before. On 28 January 1980, the USCGC *Blackthorn* (a 180-foot

buoy tender that maintained aids to navigation, performed ice breaking, and conducted search and rescue missions) tragically collided with the oil tanker *Capricorn* at the entrance to Tampa Bay, Florida. The cutter rapidly capsized, and twenty-eight members of the fifty-person crew lost their lives. The man who wrote the letter was one of the survivors.

"I got a medal," he wrote, "but there was this kid who took off his life jacket and gave it to me. He threw life jackets to the guys in the water. He took his belt and strapped open the lifejacket locker door which allowed more lifejackets to float to the surface. Then, even after most had abandoned ship, he remained on board to help our trapped shipmates. He didn't make it. I don't remember his name. He was young—straight out of boot camp—had only been on board the cutter for a few days. He's the guy who deserved the medal—not me."

The master chief spared no time or cost to find out the identity of this unknown young hero. He went back and pored through the records, interviewed former members of the crew, and narrowed the search down to nineteen-year-old Seaman Apprentice William R. Flores. The record further revealed that Flores, indeed, had behaved heroically and had not been properly recognized for his efforts.

On 16 September 2000, a formal ceremony was held in Benbrook, Texas. Among the people on hand were the Flores family, the Coast Guard's 8th District commander, and the service's highest ranking enlisted member, the Master Chief Petty Officer of the Coast Guard (who had conducted the research). There at his gravesite, in his hometown, more than twenty years after his death, William R. Flores was posthumously awarded the Coast Guard Medal—the U.S. Coast Guard's highest award for heroism.

The story of S. A. William R. Flores is a wonderful example of the culture of the U.S. Coast Guard at work. After twenty years, one man brought to the attention of an official the long forgotten and overlooked act of a very brave young man. An investigation was promptly conducted and a finding rendered. Flores's heroism was then formally recognized and his family honored in their hometown, with the proper ceremony, medal, and military personnel present. The Coast Guard's culture necessitated this action, demanded it, and made it happen.

Every organization's culture, like the Coast Guard's, defines the values, customs, and beliefs shared by its members. Usually, that culture emerges over time from the organization's specific history, geography, and philosophy. To a very large degree, culture determines how people interact with each other to achieve their mission. It also defines how people behave toward one another, how conflicts are resolved, and how clients and customers are treated.

Without a definitive culture, individual values begin to disintegrate. That's because culture nurtures the fundamental human relationship between individuals and their group. Largely an emotional element for people, culture is primarily brought to bear through character. It engenders pride and breeds loyalty and commitment. People want to be part of something larger than themselves. It is quite simply a basic human desire to want to take pride in your day-to-day work and in the organization of which you are a part.

Members of the U.S. Coast Guard view it as part of their duty not only to maintain the Coast Guard's culture, but also to strengthen it and pass it on to future generations. That's one reason why Coast Guard culture is clearly defined for every new member immediately upon entry into the service, and is reinforced and fortified throughout a career.

Whether it comes from a company commander at the Coast Guard Training Center in Cape May, New Jersey, from an instructor at the Coast Guard Academy in New London, Connecticut, or from an officer-in-charge of one of the Coast Guard stations across the country, the message is always the same. It goes something like this:

> We are engaged in an honorable profession—a noble cause. We are effective stewards of the American taxpayer's interests. We live our motto in all we do—*Semper Paratus* (Always Ready). Our bottom line is: "Service to Humanity." We are a different kind of military. We are part of the Department of Homeland Security but, during times of war (or by presidential decree), we serve with the United States Navy. In the other military services, personnel are trained to do a job that they may never perform. In the Coast Guard, we do the job we're trained to do every day. Officers provide support and direction. The chiefs and crew make it happen. Everybody is expected to give credit where credit is due. Most of all, we are a family.

We are a group of people taking care of each other. And, often, the people you meet on your first assignment become your friends for life.

We are a relatively small, tenacious, tight-knit organization. We work in small teams where there is more rapport, more communication, and less bureaucracy. We have more than two hundred stations throughout the United States and, as such, we are a decentralized organization that serves the public where the rubber meets the road. The level of day-to-day oversight from a centralized headquarters unit is minimal.

Our heritage and history is really important to us. We honor the long line of people who have come before us, who have made our service what it is today, who have made our country great. Our roots and traditions tie back to the very birth of the United States. We take pride in our past, are serious about the present, and plan for a better future.

The sea is our office, our domain. *Scientiae Cedit Mare* (The Sea Yields to Knowledge). The sea has a physical dimension. It is one of the earth's primal forces, covering three-quarters of the planet's surface. The sea also has a spiritual dimension. It is as old as time, newborn every day; eternal, but never the same. Our blood is the same salinity as seawater, yet we are so different. The sea is both cleansing and threatening; powerful, yet personal. It doesn't take much to have an impact on you. We in the Coast Guard go with a good group of people out to a place where only our training, our commitment to purpose, and our relationships with each other ensure our survival. Because the Coast Guard is inextricably intertwined with the sea, we are at one with nature—but only if we work together.

The noble cause, a different kind of military, small decentralized teams, heritage and tradition, and the sea are all well woven into the fabric of the United States Coast Guard. Equal to these, however, and perhaps even more ingrained into the culture are the core values of *Honor, Respect,* and *Devotion to Duty.* These three tenets govern behavior and conduct, are part of every individual's performance evaluation, and may not be turned off after work. They are about more than just being in the Coast Guard. Every person is expected to abide by the core values all the time, as a way of life. There are no exceptions.

HONOR

Honor is a fundamental premise in any organization. In the Coast Guard, it involves the concepts of high ethical conduct, moral behavior, honesty, integrity, trust, and doing what is right, not just what is easy. It also means honoring the traditions and principles that made the Coast Guard and the United States of America what they are today.

There are many reasons why honor is important in the Coast Guard. In order to achieve success in a team environment, for instance, trust must be developed. Therefore, it is a standing rule that team members must always be straight with each other and tell the truth both on and off duty. Because everyone is on the government's payroll, everyone must be accountable to the public trust. Unnecessary or unwarranted expenditures are not permitted, and every expenditure has to be justified with documented reasoning. Also, most logs aboard ship are still handwritten and are taken to be the truth in a court of law. This is especially important in court cases where a judge assumes the log is correct and truthful solely because it was generated on a Coast Guard cutter. It is imperative to maintain that trust and honor afforded by the courts.

Honor also becomes important in reducing risk and minimizing future mistakes. Every operation is analyzed truthfully so that, on the next case, the Coast Guard is that much better prepared. Each individual must admit when they make an error because the next time it could save a life or help a mission be successful.

RESPECT

Respect is one of the least talked about but most important values in leadership. It is important because from respect spring many other qualities, such as caring, compassion, understanding, and effective communication. In the Coast Guard, this core value embodies a fundamental respect for people. Respect for the people you serve. Respect for your shipmates. Respect for every human being you may encounter, inside or outside of the organization, from bus drivers to admirals. There is also a deep-seated belief that all people have value, despite any differences they may have. It is essentially the embodiment of the Golden Rule: Treat others as you would have them treat you. But in the Coast Guard, it is a hard and fast rule. Everyone *must* treat others fairly and with civility, consideration, and dignity.

Another important part of this core value involves respect for authority. Because the Coast Guard is a military organization, higher ranking members and their orders must be obeyed. The military salute, for instance, is actually more of an outward show of respect for authority than anything else.

Respect for yourself is also important. As one Coast Guard chief petty officer often explains to the members of his crew: "It starts with you as a person. You can't respect others until you have respect for yourself. And once you have respect for yourself, you can pass on that respect to other people."

In leadership, a healthy regard for respect directly affects an organization in at least four different ways:

1. It helps to get the job done better by facilitating teamwork. Respect is critical in a cohesive team unit. Leaders and teams, in general, can only sustain effectiveness to the extent that their relationships are based on mutual respect as well as trust.
2. It drastically reduces and often even eliminates harassment, discrimination, prejudice, insensitivity, offensive behavior, verbal abuse, and basic thoughtlessness.
3. It helps leaders understand and have a more astute awareness of the impact on people of their own behavior.
4. It facilitates and encourages open lines of communication, which, in turn, fosters caring and compassion for all people.

At the Coast Guard training facility in Cape May, New Jersey, one company commander tells new recruits this about the core value of respect:

> The person on your left or your right might be the person who saves your life. That person might be tying off your safety line or looking out for you. At boat stations we spend a lot of close time together, sometimes 48–96 hours before we get under way. We *must* have mutual respect for each other.
>
> One of our duties is to recover the remains of people after tragic plane crashes at sea. We try to be as dignified and respectful as possible so that families can have some closure.
>
> We also have a responsibility for illegal immigration on the water. When you pick up immigrants off a makeshift raft, you must show them respect. At the very least, you should show them respect just for trying to do something to improve their lives, to help their families, their friends, themselves.

Even if they berate you or yell at you, you must retain your respect for them. Because if you can disrespect one person, then it becomes too easy for you to come up with a reason to disrespect someone else.

DEVOTION TO DUTY

Devotion to duty is the moral obligation to place the accomplishment of assigned tasks before individual needs, considerations, or possible advancements. It's the basic acceptance of responsibility, accountability, and commitment to doing the job. It means taking pride in what you do. And in the Coast Guard, it also involves a higher calling. "In our organization," says one admiral, "we exist to serve our country and its citizens. We serve with pride. We are devoted to preserving life."

This core value, when exhibited by every person in an organization, can result in amazing achievements. It tends to create an organization of doers. No one ever says to a colleague, "Hey, you need to slow down, because you're making the rest of us look bad." Rather, everybody works at maximum speed and efficiency. They are committed to showing up for work on time and staying as long as is necessary to get the job done. They are always at their station, always alert, and always attending to their duties.

Devotion to duty often leads to individuals making uncommon personal sacrifices so that the highest standards of the organization can be maintained. It can bring out the best in people of integrity. And it is one reason why so many members of the U.S. Coast Guard, over the course of their careers, have saved a life.

In the fall of 1998, the 102-person crew of the USCGC *Harriet Lane* was engaged on a counter-narcotics mission in the southern part of the Caribbean Sea. At mid-day, a Navy ship (three times the size of the 270-foot *Harriet Lane*) pulled along side for refueling. Protocol for this operation was specific and yet routine. The crew had done it many times before. The two ships were moving on the water at the same speed, connected by an 8-inch fueling line attached to a cable. Conditions in the engine room are restricted. For safety reasons, the mains and generators must be running all the time, at all costs. Engine room personnel are taught that, in the event of a fuel line leak, their duty is to do whatever it takes to stop that fuel from spraying on the hot main. Fuel on the hot main means that an explosion could occur, the cutter could catch fire, and could possibly be pulled into the side of the Navy ship. In that event, all personnel on both ships would be in mortal danger.

About halfway through the operation, a high-pressure fuel line burst underneath the deck plate of the engine room. Fuel immediately started spraying everywhere, and the engine room began to fill with the mist of fuel spray. Without a second thought, a twenty-two-year-old machinery technician second class named Mark immediately jumped underneath the deck plate and wrapped himself around the hole in the burst fuel line. Diesel fuel sprayed onto his chest, into his face, and saturated his clothing. None of the systems could be shut down until the cutter did an emergency breakaway from the Navy fueler. A considerable amount of time passed before the main fuel line could be shut down to stop the leak. Mark hung on the entire time.

Nothing caught fire due to the fact that this one young man had made himself a human bandage. If he had not put his life on the line, the engine room almost certainly would have caught fire and endangered all of his ship-mates and the crew of the Navy ship. As the ship's fire chief foamed down the engine room, Mark was carried topside. He had fuel in his eyes, in his throat, and in his stomach. He was temporarily blinded, was having difficulty breathing, and was vomiting. His shipmates took meticulous care of their colleague, tending to him day and night. After three or four days, Mark's chief found him back at his post in the engine room. He was good to go.

THE COAST GUARD ON LEADERSHIP

Define the Culture and Live the Values

- Remember that an organization's culture is primarily brought to bear through character. It engenders pride and breeds loyalty and commitment.
- Decrease the separation between executives and everybody else.
- Make your organization like a family—a group of people taking care of one another.
- Work in small teams where there is more rapport, more communication, and less bureaucracy.
- Minimize the level of day-to-day oversight from headquarters.
- Honor is a fundamental premise in any organization. It reduces risk and minimizes future mistakes.
- In order to achieve success, trust must be developed in every member of the team.
- Have your organization revolve around a fundamental respect for people. Make sure that everyone is treated fairly and with civility, consideration, and dignity.
- From respect spring caring, compassion, understanding, and dignity.
- Respect in an organization:
    1. Facilitates teamwork
    2. Reduces discrimination and harassment
    3. Helps leaders understand the impact of their own behavior
    4. Facilitates open lines of communication.
- Devotion to duty can result in amazing achievements and can bring out the best in people of integrity.
- Create an organization of doers where everybody works at maximum speed and efficiency.

Chapter 2

Select the Best

Because of our mission, we have to pick strong people in the first
place—people who are honest, who have not only a respect
for authority but also the ability to work in a team
environment. We all end up working beside
each other one way or another.

—Coast Guard recruiter

Character, the foundation of leadership, is also the
foundation of the U.S. Coast Guard.

M any large organizations have so many vacancies to fill that they end
up settling for the first warm body that walks through the door. But
not the U.S. Coast Guard.

Coasties have important missions to accomplish. Every member of the
team must be able to contribute to the cause. They must be able to perform
multiple tasks, and they must become leaders in whatever position they

st Guard oper-
nited States. A
st high school
r-year college
demy, located
my not only
training for
leaders, and
leaders.
d Academy
didates, of
s and SAT
. To deter-
rong lead-
nterviews.
plication
s to serve
ve been
sible evi-
n school
predis-
ent of a
school.
ecause
many
a job
hers.
uard
very
e're
hing
past

try
ice
of
ol

ınot meet these objectives. Therefore,
process.

ulous and relentless in their search for
ınow through a hundred or more appli-
that will be seriously considered. As one
ıtes: "Because of our mission, we have to
ıce, people who are honest, who have not
the ability to work in a team environment.
each other one way or another. We all end
d we all have to be able to pull together into
nperative to choose people who already have
to more naturally fit in."

arch for people who have a predisposition for
the seven individual qualities they seek when

ho are bright, curious, and creative tend to rise
ınd innovative ways to succeed.

t people with abundant energy tend to get more
occasion in a fast-paced, multi-mission organiza-

cure people who are at peace with themselves tend
a team environment. They also tend to attract fol-

ng: People who are adaptable, flexible, and able to
quickly are often natural leaders who tend to per-
dynamic environment.

Caring individuals with great heart are well suited to
ırd's humanitarian mission. They also tend to foster
on and generate followers.

h a bias toward action: Results-oriented, persevering
ıre the people who make things happen in any organiza-
courage often inspires courage in others.

Honesty, integrity, and trustworthiness are fundamental to
ıization. Character, the foundation of leadership, is also the
on of the U.S. Coast Guard.

In order to find and attract people for its enlisted ranks, the Coa
ates dozens of recruiting stations scattered throughout the U
heavy emphasis is placed on signing up people who have at lea
diplomas. Those high school grads interested in pursuing a fou
degree are invited to apply to the United States Coast Guard Aca
in New London, Connecticut. Established in 1876, the acade
serves as a fully accredited university, it also provides specific
career officers of the Coast Guard. The academy exists to shape
those who graduate, without exception, are expected to *become*

Unlike the nation's other military academies, the Coast Guar
does not have congressional appointments for admission. Can
course, must meet high academic requirements (including grade
scores), and they must also pass muster on a variety of other fronts
mine whether applicants have the seven qualities determined for st
ership predisposition, the Coast Guard conducts extensive personal i
Heavy emphasis is placed on letters of recommendation. The ap
process requires individual essays relating why the candidate want
with the Coast Guard. Priority is often given to people who h
involved in charity work in their local communities because it is tan
dence of an individual reaching out toward others. In addition, hig
participation in sports is viewed as a positive factor in an individual's
position to work in a team environment. It is not unusual for 75 perc
cadet class at the Academy to have participated in varsity sports in high

In later years, people often become attracted to the Coast Guard b
of the humanitarian mission. After spending years in corporations,
are searching to add something of significance in their lives, to have
that really makes a difference, or simply to do something that helps o
"It's meaningful work," relates one thirty-five-year-old Coast C
reservist from Los Angeles. "If you're going to spend a weekend
month, you want to do something that matters. In the Coast Guard,
training for something that is done every day on the job, not for somet
that might happen. And even though we're a military service, the C
Guard is more about preserving life than taking it."

Members of the Coast Guard Reserve come from all over the cour
and from all professions. Each month, training for new reserves takes pl
at Cape May, New Jersey. And each new class is likely to be composed
a cross section of the nation: a deputy sheriff from Tampa, a border patr

officer from Seattle, a special agent with U.S. Customs in Chicago, an insurance agent from New York City, a registered nurse from northern Michigan, a pharmacist from Indianapolis, to name a few.

After being in the Coast Guard for a while, scores of reservists will point out that they like not only the mission, but also other things they had not expected to find. Things like the teamwork, the esprit de corps, the relative lack of oversight from headquarters, the smaller and more limited bureaucracy, the quality of the people, and the fact that people are more interested in *doing* their jobs than in *protecting* their jobs.

Many Coast Guard reservists have formerly served on active duty and in the reserves of the Navy, Marines, Army, and Air Force. One forty-something former Marine who wanted to join the reserves in order to make a difference interviewed with all the military services before making his choice. "When I got to the Coast Guard," he related, "it was more like I was interviewing for a job. They were selecting me as well as me selecting them. I liked that. They really quizzed me about my skills, my background, and what I thought I could offer to the Coast Guard. I never got that from the other services. It was obvious that the Coast Guard was not just looking for warm bodies. That's one reason I accepted a position when it was offered."

Selecting the best people for your team greatly increases your organization's chance of success. Obviously, leaders who surround themselves with high achievers will be able to get more done with fewer people. And when people know that the job won't get done unless they do it themselves, they will often rise to the occasion and perform amazing tasks. Young people, especially, fit into this trend.

In most organizations, young people entering the work force have to start out at the bottom and wait years before they can actually do something that makes a difference. In the Coast Guard, however, recruits sign up for terms of three to six years, take an oath to support the Constitution of the United States, and then are assigned a position where they have an immediate impact. It's not a matter of "if," it's a matter of "when" and "where." Every day they will wake up and say, "I don't know exactly what I'm going to be doing today, but I very well may be saving lives."

After making it through the Training Center at Cape May, Patrick was assigned to a cutter off the Pacific coast. Originally from Michigan and in his early twenties, he had spent a year working his way through art school and studying graphic design. But when he ran out of money, Patrick decided to join the Coast Guard for a couple of years and try to save up. Having been an athlete in high school, he knew he could pass the physical standards to become an aviation survival technician. So he put his request in, was accepted, went through training, and was sent to Kodiak, Alaska.

Within a few days of Patrick's arrival, his new station received a distress call from a fishing vessel about two hundred fifty miles off the coast of the Aleutian Islands in the Bering Sea. Five minutes later, Patrick was headed out to sea in a rescue helicopter with his crew, which consisted of two officers (pilot and copilot) and two enlisted personnel (flight mechanic and Patrick, the aviation survival technician). Once they were airborne, they received more detailed information about the fishing vessel. It was reported that a man had gotten his arm caught in a loop and had been jerked overboard in rough seas. When his fellow crew members pulled him back in, they found that his arm was almost severed. Everybody in the helicopter crew knew that if they could not rescue this individual and get him to a hospital, he would probably bleed to death.

After several hours of travel time, the rescue helicopter reached the boat. It was at night, in the middle of a wind-laced snowstorm with 25-foot seas. While the pilot held the aircraft steady and hovered overhead, the flight mechanic, using the motorized hoist, lowered Patrick down toward the boat. Suddenly, a big wave propelled the boat's steel girder rigging right toward him. Patrick's body wrapped around the girder like a rag doll and then he was flung away. His line started swinging wildly from the helicop-ter—and immediately, the flight mechanic hauled him back in.

"Are you all right?" asked the pilot. "I was afraid we might have killed you. These conditions may just be too dangerous to get you down on the deck of that boat."

"I'm okay," responded the young man. "A little bruised, but okay."

As Patrick composed himself, he knew the call was his to make. If he did not want to try again, he knew his team would call off the mission and return to base. But that would also mean that the injured man on the boat below would probably die. "Let's try it again," he said.

The crew then began to resurvey the situation. "Listen," said Patrick, "this time, don't take me in from up high. Take me in along the water on the horizontal. I might get dunked a few times, but then I'll only have to deal with one dimension. Bring me up beside the boat and then just plop me on the railing. That way I'm sure not to swing into the girder again."

That approach worked. Patrick got dunked a couple of times, but finally made it onto the fishing vessel, where he secured the line so that the litter basket could be lowered down. Then he went into the cabin to check out the victim. The rest of the boat's crew had him spread out on a table with an air splint on his damaged arm. There was blood everywhere, and Patrick knew there was no time to waste. They packaged up the patient, put him in the litter, and gave the okay sign for the flight mechanic to lift him up into the helicopter.

As the victim was raised and secured into the helicopter, Patrick looked up from the boat. The spotlight on the underside of the chopper was almost blinding. The snow was blowing sideways and the boat was moving up and down on the 25-foot waves. "How in the world am I going to get back into that thing," he wondered silently.

The flight mechanic lowered the line and tried to pull Patrick up as quickly as possible. However, Patrick immediately began to swing way out to the side. Then, as he was about 50 feet below the aircraft, he felt a jerk. The cable had gotten caught on part of the landing gear and then had broken free. That started him swinging insanely back and forth, like Tarzan on a vine. This was not the way it was supposed to go. Scared to death, Patrick thought, "Well, this is it. Here I am a hundred feet up in the air and hanging from a line thinner than my pinky finger. The steel girder is going to hit me again and that'll be it."

But the flight crew was determined not to let that happen. The pilot maneuvered the aircraft away from the boat, while the flight mechanic increased the speed on the line to get their buddy back into the chopper as fast as possible. Finally, they got him in.

"Are you all right?" asked the pilot. "We were worried about you."

Patrick gave the "thumbs up" sign and said: "Rock on, sir."

With that, the pilot made a beeline for the nearest medical facility, which was in Cold Bay, Alaska.

The victim lost his arm, but survived. And Patrick knew the effort had been worth it.

The Coast Guard on Leadership

Select the Best

- Don't hire the first warm body that walks through the door.
- Hire people capable of performing multiple tasks—people who can become leaders in whatever positions they may hold.
- Search for people who have a predisposition for strong leadership, for those who possess these seven qualities:
    1. Intelligence
    2. High energy
    3. Self-confidence
    4. Continual learning
    5. Compassion
    6. Courage with a bias toward action
    7. Character.
- Look for people who have had experience participating in a team sport.
- Make sure potential recruits understand that they will perform meaningful work if they join your team.
- People enjoy working in an organization with teamwork, esprit de corps, little oversight from headquarters, a limited bureaucracy, and coworkers who are people of character.
- Selecting the best people for your team will allow you to get more done with fewer people and will greatly increase your organization's chance of success.

Chapter 3

Promote Team over Self

When you get to your first station, you will become part of a small,
tight-knit unit. Whether it's a helicopter crew, a boarding team,
or a cutter crew, teamwork is fundamental. . . . So
remember: you're in this together! You've got to
trust the person next to you, behind you,
and in front of you.

—Coast Guard company commander,
to new recruits

You only swim as fast as the slowest member of the group.

—Boot camp training maxim

"Okay, everybody," barked the company commander. "I want all of you to
fall out and be back here in formation within zero-two minutes—*in full
working blue uniform!*" This order was issued during the first week in boot
camp after a calisthenics workout, when everybody in Romeo Company

(120 people) was outside and dressed in gym clothes.

"Geez, is he kidding?"

"There's no way we can do that!"

"No way!"

And they were not able to do it. They didn't even come close. People straggled out one at a time over the next fifteen minutes.

"Pitiful!" roared the company commander. "Pitiful! When you guys learn to work together, you'll be able to do it. And I'm going to ask you to do that at least once a week. I'll give you a hint: Work in your own group of eight. But for now, hit the grass and give me ten! All of you! Now!"

Back in the barracks, each group of eight had a powwow and tried to figure out a way to do it.

"Either we have to start coming together or we're going to be in the grass our entire time here, and nobody likes being in the grass."

"He said we should work together."

"Yeah, and in our own group."

"How can we speed this up? Who's good at what?"

Within a couple of weeks, people were buttoning up each other's jackets, buffing each other's shoes, polishing smudges off brass belt buckles, brushing the lint off shirts and jackets, and tying each other's ties. In the fourth week, one group made it out in the prescribed two minutes, the others were late. But there was no slack from the company commander.

"Only eight of you made it out in time, everybody else was late," he bellowed. "Hit the grass!"

After hours, all of Romeo Company got together. The fast group coached the other groups on how to increase their speed. By the sixth week, everybody was changed and back in line inside of two minutes.

"Congratulations, Romeo," said the company commander with a smile. "You're finally learning to become a team."

They call it early indoctrination for recruits, but it's better known as boot camp. The Coast Guard Training Center at Cape May, New Jersey, runs 4,300 new recruits through an eight-week program each year.

All new cadets at the Coast Guard Academy in New London go through a similar program (called "swab summer") the summer before they begin classes. Essentially, everybody receives ground-floor training in the rudiments of seamanship and the military, and, of course, all are exposed to the organization's core values of Honor, Respect, and Devotion to Duty. But the major emphasis taught, by far, is the concept of team over self.

People come into the Coast Guard from all over the country, with different backgrounds, different expectations, and different values. They are superb individuals who excel at individual accomplishment. For many, it doesn't come naturally to act as part of a team. Yet everyone must be brought to the point where they focus on the group first and themselves second, because teamwork is the way the U.S. Coast Guard functions.

But how in the world does the Coast Guard change in only eight weeks what it took eighteen or more years to build up? In a well-thought-through and evolved process, all new recruits are first made to look alike. Their hair is cut short, and they are issued identical uniforms. Second, everything is taken away from them: their stereos, televisions, computers, video games, even their parents. All they're left with is the hearts in their bodies, the air in their lungs, and their classmates. Then they are placed in a situation where they're forced to work with each other. All live and sleep together in very close quarters. Beds are stacked three high. There is little time to dress, shower, make up bunks, and so on. The situation forces everyone to think about how they're going to get things done with a lot of people constantly milling around.

The recruits next learn structure, responsibility, attention to detail, and discipline. They learn to accomplish tasks as an entire company or as subdivisions of a company. They learn, for example, how to march together, how to move from point A to point B as a group. If one person gets it wrong, the entire company has to march for an hour as punishment. People who can't take the discipline are weeded out. Natural leaders rise to the top. After a short while, nearly everyone becomes comfortable with the discipline and routine. They begin to build loyalty and trust. And they learn to depend on one another.

All through the process, instructors constantly emphasize the fact that, at the operational leading edge of the Coast Guard, everyone functions as part of a team.

"When you get to your first station," says one company commander, "you will become part of a small, tight-knit unit. Whether it's a helicopter crew, a boarding team, or a cutter crew enforcing the law or engaging in search and rescue, teamwork is fundamental. The idea is to promote maximum efficiency at the delivery point of service. Never forget the consequences of failing to work in a team. If you're on a helicopter, it could be a smoking hole in the ground. On a cutter, a life lost. So remember—you're in this together! You've got to trust the person next to you, the one behind you, and the one in front of you."

Company commanders also strategically link to their instruction stories of Coast Guard history, tradition, and heroism that bring to life the value of teamwork. A small boat crew working together to save a life might be used as an example, or the Coast Guard's involvement with the Navy and Marines in the D-Day landing at Normandy during World War II. The youthful Medal of Honor winner Douglas Munro saving the lives of countless stranded Marines during the battle of Guadalcanal, or a reminder of how the Coast Guard has been there every single time Americans have been called to defend their nation, working as part of a larger team with the Navy, Marines, Army, and Air Force.

Every organization can't have a boot camp designed to instill teamwork in their employees. But every organization *can* create an indoctrination program that instills buy-in from the very beginning, where important beliefs are preached. "This is our culture, and these are the principles we live by." "This is our mission." "This is how we work together." "This is our history." "These are the people who came before you. They are our legacy. We are not going to let them down."

And it is certainly appropriate for every organization to teach the key elements of successful teamwork. In addition to instilling the core values of Honor, Respect, and Devotion to Duty (which, of course, facilitate teamwork), it is the goal of the Coast Guard to have each individual who graduates from the early indoctrination programs believe in, and be trained in, the following five key elements of teamwork.

1. Focus and attention to detail: A fine-tuned attention to the task at hand without allowing distractions to get in the way; a belief that little things can make a difference in critical situations; an understanding that no job is insignificant.

2. <u>Personal accountability</u>: The understanding that each of us is responsible for our part of the team effort. If the task isn't performed, the job doesn't get done and the team will be unsuccessful. This involves having the discipline to perform a particular task and accepting personal responsibility for one's own behavior and performance.

3. <u>Caring</u>: Compassion for the dignity and humanity of all people, especially team members and those being served. Compassion involves the belief that everyone is special and has value; the ability to place oneself in the shoes of another and feel what they feel; the capacity to care about one's coworkers and one's own work on a daily basis.

4. <u>Selflessness and collective responsibility</u>: The understanding that if one member of the team fails, the entire team fails. This entails the belief that "you only swim as fast as the slowest member of the group"; the humility of not singling yourself out but, rather, recognizing the team effort; and the understanding that, on average, a team achieves 33 percent more than a group of individuals acting separately.

5. <u>Pride</u>: Self-esteem, dignity, and enjoyment in working with the team, and in the collective accomplishment of the group. It means thinking enough of your job to maintain the very highest standard of excellence, and being proud to be a member of the U. S. Coast Guard.

In Alaska, the crews that fly the big planes, the C-130s, know their role is primarily one of support. They support the cutters when they're out enforcing fisheries boundaries by flying patrol patterns. They help guide helicopters to search and rescue sites by flying search patterns and pinpointing precise locations. And they fly supplies in and out of remote LORAN (Long Range Aids to Navigation) stations where Coast Guard members are posted for up to a year at a time.

Regularly, however, they also fly out to the Maritime Boundary Line, where Russia and the United States have divided up an exclusive economic zone. Their primary role here is to ensure that everybody fishing on the Russian side is staying on the Russian side. And you can bet your bottom dollar that if the C-130s were not there, foreign trawlers would not be respecting the line. Those huge trawlers can collect a lot of fish in a short amount of time.

A typical mission takes off from Kodiak, Alaska, on a twenty-five-hundred-mile round trip that lasts between eight and ten hours. They spend two to three hours flying the two hundred fifty–mile line obtaining all the names and numbers of the ships. It's a fairly high-risk environment, flying at an altitude of two hundred to three hundred feet, banking back and forth at forty-five-degree angles. The seven-member crew consists of a pilot, copilot, flight engineer, navigator, radioman, and two technicians. Their mission is to obtain the name and registration numbers of the ships they encounter (usually around fifty to seventy), and determine if they are fishing on the proper side of the line.

That sounds easy, but when you're a long way from home with limited fuel and time, you have to be extremely efficient. That's where the teamwork comes in. All seven members of the crew are involved in a well-orchestrated routine. They call it "doing the dance."

The ships do not fish in straight lines. They're scattered all over the place. So the pilot chooses the target and maneuvers the plane in and out, setting up the next two or three targets down the road, just as one would do when shooting a good game of pool. The flight engineer and one of the technicians are stationed by windows on either side of the plane. They are the ones who yell out the numbers. But they cannot see the ships until the plane is almost upon them. If they are distracted even for a moment, they will miss their opportunity to see the number.

The pilot calls out: "Next boat! Fifteen seconds on the right (or left). Okay, here it comes. Ten seconds, five, four three, two, one. *Now!*"

The copilot calls out, "Mark!" as he hits a button on the computer and freezes the boat's position.

Everybody else is quiet. If everything is going right, you're not going to hear anything. There is trust in the silence. Everybody knows the unwritten rule: "If you see it, say nothing. If you don't, speak up."

The navigator pushes another button on the computer and marks the boat's position relative to the line. The flight engineer (or a technician) yells out the boat numbers. The other technician writes down the numbers on the information sheets. The radioman then takes all the information and pulls it together. If a fishing vessel is found on the U.S. side, he immediately radios the nearest Coast Guard cutter (one is usually cruising the line somewhere). The cutter will then move in and cite the violator. If there is no cutter nearby, the radioman will immediately go into the "hot pursuit" checklist, where they document all the key data and transmit it back to Kodiak for future legal enforcement.

In November 2001, a Russian trawler was detected more than four hundred yards over the line. A Coast Guard cutter was sent in, and an arrest was made. The incident made international headlines. The owners of the trawler were heavily fined by both the U.S. and Russian governments.

The Bering Sea and Gulf of Alaska are estimated to provide 40–60 percent of the protein biomass in the world. Alaskan fisheries are a $7 billion–$10 billion business. Maritime law enforcement is one of the missions of the Coast Guard. All seven members of the C-130 crew take pride in "doing the dance." They know that if they weren't on hand, the line would be violated frequently. "It's our job," they say. "And we know it's important for the country."

The Coast Guard on Leadership

Promote Team over Self

- Have your organization function in a team environment. People will be more productive by far. They will also be happier.
- For many people of high individual achievement, it is not natural to act as part of a team. Teamwork has to be taught.
- Create an early indoctrination program in your organization that instills buy-in from the beginning of each individual's participation.
- Teach new employees about the organization's mission, how people work together, and about the organization's history and legacy.
- After working together for a while, people become accustomed to discipline and routine. They begin to build loyalty and trust. And they learn to depend on one another.
- Teach the five key elements of teamwork:
    1. Focus and attention to detail
    2. Personal accountability
    3. Caring
    4. Selflessness and collective responsibility
    5. Pride.
- Remember that you only swim as fast as the slowest member of the group.
- Understand that, on average, a team achieves 33 percent more than a group of individuals acting separately.

Chapter 4

Instill a Commitment to Excellence

The Coast Guard does not simply rely on the natural inclinations of its
members to work hard. It also puts in place a full-fledged,
organization-wide program related to quality and
excellence in all work performed and all services
rendered. Everyone is coached to operate
with the highest possible standards.

In whatever job we do, we do the very best we can—*every single
time.* Either we do it top-notch, or we don't do it at all.

—Unofficial motto of the Coast Guard

Scott is a seasoned pilot at one of the largest stations in the Coast Guard.
He has direct involvement in search and rescue, law enforcement, marine
patrols, and aids to navigation. He has to stay proficient in training for pilot-
ing and emergency procedures. He stands six duties every month, at least

one a week, for a twenty-four-hour period. Most of the time, he flies one or two days each week. Sometimes, during the busy season, he's in the air every day. He has been awarded the Distinguished Flying Cross for heroism.

Once in a while, though, Scott has to tell his boss that he can't fly because of his other job. You see, Scott is also the comptroller of the base. He oversees a $7 million annual budget and a $20 million aviation parts warehouse.

"This money stuff takes a lot of time," he says. "I'm usually in the office on off-days. Every minute of my time is filled. I work twenty-four/seven. That's my job. And you know what? I love it."

Teamwork is the *way* Coast Guard people achieve their missions. *What* they do is defined by their commitment to excellence. And there's only one way an organization with so few active members and such a broad-ranging mission as the U. S. Coast Guard can achieve so much: Not only does every person have to be committed to excellence, they all have to contribute. *Everybody* has to wear more than one hat.

In Massachusetts, a petty officer in a small boat station is not just a boat coxswain. He's also a boarding officer, the officer of the day (when on duty), and a small arms instructor. He has responsibility for the planning of all schedules, and runs the LEIS (Law Enforcement Information System).

In Texas, the crew of a buoy tender do a lot more than just tend buoys. They also look after numerous lighthouses, join in search and rescue operations, and respond to reports of pollution.

In Hawaii, one enlisted chief petty officer is a plumber, a carpenter, a welder, and a fabricator. He's also in charge of chemical and biological training and has responsibility for related equipment on board ships. And he has five people who report to him.

In many large organizations, if people are asked to perform a job with which they are not familiar, a typical response may be: "That's not in my job description." But in the Coast Guard, active members without formal training in computer use may be handed a new laptop and asked to perform a new task. And, almost always, they will find a way to get the job done. This is where the Coast Guard philosophy of recruiting individuals with superior talent really pays off. Every employee can handle more than one job. In fact, most thrive on the additional responsibility.

The Coast Guard, however, does not simply rely on the natural inclinations of its members to work hard. It also puts in place a full-fledged, organization-wide program related to quality and excellence in all work performed and all services rendered. Everyone is coached to operate with the highest possible standards. Not only are they extensively schooled in their areas of expertise, they are trained to take the initiative and fix things that need fixing, even if they are not given specific orders to do so. For example, when Coasties find something broken—a process or a piece of equipment—they are asked to find out why it broke and then fix it so it won't break again. Everyone is encouraged to take the opportunity to dissect what they are involved in, find ways to improve it, and leave it in the best condition possible.

There are also standardized training programs that are consistent across the organization. Helicopter crews, for instance, operate with the exact same procedures whether they're in New Orleans or Clearwater. A pilot or flight mechanic who is transferred from Los Angeles to Atlantic City will be immediately familiar with the modus operandi. Regarding relationships, the newly transferred Coasties are immediately accepted because they are members of the Coast Guard family, because everyone knows they have undergone the same training, and because a core value of the organization is Respect.

When Coast Guard personnel arrive on the scene, they are expected to be competent in their field and perform with excellence. If they are not able to do their jobs up to Coast Guard standards, they are subject to a deselection process by members of their immediate team. "We only have twenty-one people here," explains one member of a small cutter crew. "That's all we have. Everybody has to rely on everybody else to do their jobs. When we get somebody in who's not responsible, or who can't cut it, people in the group will stand up and say, 'I don't feel safe with this guy.' We work without a safety net here. If a mistake is made, someone could get hurt, or even worse, killed. No one is treated unfairly, and we do not operate on a fear factor. But you have a job to do, and if you are negligent in your job, and it happens too many times, and there are no signs of improvement, then you're out. That's the way it is. That's the way it has to be."

Excellence in the Coast Guard is all about providing efficient and effective service on America's oceans, lakes, and inland waterways, environments that are often extremely hostile. As one district commander explained to all personnel under his authority: "The sea can be intolerant of carelessness; mistakes can be deadly. Accordingly, we must have an unrelenting focus on operational excellence. We must be committed to quality and excellence in everything we do. Quality, empowerment, and continuous improvement are essential to our success."

He further pointed out that when an organization instills a commitment to excellence in all work and services, it also trusts its people to exhibit integrity.

We must provide an excellent return on investment to the American public. We must always ask ourselves: "Is this how I would want my tax dollars spent?" Americans have confidence in our ability, trust in our integrity, and faith in our dedication. They expect us to succeed under the direst of circumstances when no others can. They count on us to rescue them from harm, to protect the environment, to keep waterways open and safe, and to enforce laws firmly, fairly, and with respect for our citizens. At the same time, they expect us to manage their money properly and efficiently.

There are more than two hundred Coast Guard stations around the country that continually try to do more with less and routinely perform with excellence. But in the fall of 2000, one senior chief petty officer had the courage to stand up and explain to his superiors that his small boat station on the coast of Massachusetts simply was not able to meet Coast Guard standards.

His assigned geographic area ranged from fifty miles seaward of Nantucket all the way to Martha's Vineyard. His unit was responsible for enforcing every federal law that applied to any vessel operating in that vicinity, from having the proper number of children's life jackets to not allowing a certain type of sea turtle on board. They were also responsible for boating safety, fisheries enforcement, environmental pollution prevention and response, and search and rescue. The senior chief had twenty-five people in his unit and four boats (44-foot motor lifeboat, 47-foot motor lifeboat, 41-foot utility boat, and 21-foot rigid hull inflatable).

They had performed splendidly in the thick of recovery operations after the crashes of John F. Kennedy, Jr.'s private plane and Egypt Air flight 990 in 1999. Sorely taxed by those events, however, the unit experienced a number of equipment failures resulting from greater than normal use. At the same time, it faced an unusually high personnel turnover ratio (60 percent), which resulted in increased workloads and reduced levels of experience.

"There were certain law enforcement operations that we were just unable to perform," explained the senior chief. "We didn't have enough qualified people. So I stood up and said to my boss: 'I cannot do this anymore. I'm not going to piecemeal it and do a half-baked job. Here's why I can't.' And I explained the reasons. I pretty much asked to be left alone to do nothing but train, perform search and rescue missions, and respond to national emergencies. I asked for a period of six months in which to turn things around."

The senior chief's captain supported the action, as did the commanding admiral of the First District and the flag officers at Coast Guard headquarters in Washington, D.C. As a result, he was given eight months instead of six to organize and train his unit and get it back up to snuff. During that time, the flag officers studied the situation very closely and implemented some organization-wide changes to reduce the risk of the same thing happening elsewhere.

Leaders in any organization can institute formal quality programs. They can train and coach employees to perform with excellence. And they can create a culture that weeds out poor performers. But how in the world can a top-flight organization motivate people to perform with excellence when they believe their jobs are boring and filled with endless hours of drudgery? How do leaders in the Coast Guard, for example, motivate a communication engineer who sits for hours on end waiting for an emergency SOS on the high seas, a cook who prepares the crew's meals on an icebreaker, or a mechanic who works with helicopter engines on the hangar deck of an air station?

Coast Guard leaders do it in two simple steps. First, they instill in each person the value of the job they are performing. And second, they do so personally.

_____

It was New Year's Eve, 1979. Gordy was only nineteen years old at the time. He was less than a year out of Cape May, stationed on the island of

Okinawa, Japan, and had generator watch. In his mind, it didn't get much worse than that.

Gordy had left boot camp with excitement and enthusiasm. But then it wore off. Now, on a night when he thought he should be out celebrating with family and friends, he was feeling sorry for himself. He was homesick and lonely, and wondering what in the heck he was doing in this outfit with this cruddy job. Once every hour he would get up and read the gauges, maybe wipe off some oil residue. And for what?

Then, at about ten o'clock that evening, Gordy's boss, a senior chief petty officer, walked in.

"How's it going, Gordy?"

"Well, I hope to God I'm not sitting here this time next year doing this meaningless work," responded the young man in frustration.

The senior chief petty officer then sat down and had a heart-to-heart talk with his charge. "It's not going to be like this forever," he said. "You may not understand the importance of what you're doing here, but let me explain it more fully. Looking after this generator is extremely important to our mission—extremely important."

"Come on, senior chief. Don't put me on."

"Gordy, we are in charge of running this LORAN station. Ships on the high seas, all across the Pacific Rim from Tokyo to Australia to California, depend on our signal towers to plot their courses and guide their way. We run on generator power. If all the teeth on these gears aren't hitting on all cylinders, we're going to be in trouble. If the generator goes down, we lose power. If we lose power, the signal goes down. If the signal goes down, ships can't navigate properly. That can give rise to perilous conditions, especially at night or in stormy weather. Lives can be lost. Our mission is to keep these signal towers operational, to make sure that lives are not lost. Right now, this is where you are in the entire process: You are the only person on duty who is qualified to keep this generator running and to fix it quickly should it stop running. You, son, are the only person between life and death for thousands of people on thousands of ships at sea. They're counting on the Coast Guard to keep this signal going. Right now, you are the Coast

Guard to them. Right now, they're counting on *you*."

That night, the senior chief spent three hours just talking with the young Coastie. At midnight, they popped open a couple of sodas and toasted the New Year. Gordy got the message. He was profoundly affected by it. And he went on to serve in the United States Coast Guard for more than twenty years.

THE COAST GUARD ON LEADERSHIP

Instill a Commitment to Excellence

- Have people in your organization wear more than one hat. Eliminate the phrase "That's not in my job description."
- Really talented people will find a way to get the job done. They thrive on additional responsibility.
- Do not rely solely on the natural inclinations of your people to get the job done. Put in place an organization-wide program related to quality and excellence in all work performed and services rendered.
- Coach everyone to operate at the highest possible standards.
- Train people to fix things that need fixing. Encourage them to dissect what they are involved in, find ways to improve it, and leave it in the best condition possible.
- If people are not able to perform their jobs up to your standards, permit a deselection process to be initiated by members of their immediate team.
- A commitment to excellence is all about providing efficient and effective service delivery to clients in their own environment.
- Quality, empowerment, and continuous improvement are essential to success.
- When an organization instills a commitment to excellence in all work and services, it also trusts its people to behave with integrity.
- In whatever job you do, do the very best you can, *every single time.* Either do it top-notch, or don't do it at all.
- Instill in each person the value of the job they are performing. And do so personally.

PART TWO   Focus on People

Chapter 5

Eliminate the Frozen Middle

Coast Guard chiefs are like white blood cells clustering around a disease
in the human body. They don't stop until the body is cured. In a
very real sense, they are absolutely critical to the health
and well-being of the organization.

—Commandant of Cadets, U.S. Coast Guard Academy

It's kind of like exercising your right to free speech. If something's
not right, as a good citizen, you have to stand up and say
something about it. So long as we're reasonable, the
organization supports our actions.

—Coast Guard command master chief

In every organization, there is a "frozen middle." The larger the organization, the thicker and more iced-up it is. It's composed of the middle managers who, technically, run everything. And yet, ninety-nine times out of a hundred, they are the people who are the most resistant to change. In essence, they're "frozen" into inaction and inertia. "This is the way I've been doing it for twenty years," they say. "I don't see any reason to change. It's comfortable the way it is. I want a career. I want to get promoted. So

I'm not going to take any risks. Better to do nothing than risk losing it all."

The conventional way for a business corporation to break up the frozen middle is to use "ice picks" in localized areas. The senior executives chip away from above. They want to make things happen so they can garner larger profits. And lower echelon staff chip away from below. They want to get things done for their customers. But the Coast Guard approaches things in a different way. Rather than chipping away with ice picks, it effectively eliminates the frozen middle by melting it completely and keeping things thawed out.

And how do you melt ice? You heat it up.

Scientifically, the process of heating agitates electrons that, as a result of the agitation, turn ice into water, leaving a fluid system where everything moves—up, down, and sideways.

In the Coast Guard, there are more than thirty-one thousand enlisted men and women, making up more than 80 percent of active duty personnel. They are led by chief petty officers and chief warrant officers, the noncommissioned officers of the organization. And when you ask any person in the Coast Guard (officer or enlisted) who the agitators are, you will receive an immediate and consistent answer: "the chiefs."

Chiefs bring to the Coast Guard a combination of skills and knowledge, tenure, and a school-of-hard-knocks kind of leadership. Along with the junior commissioned officer corps, they compose the middle management layer of the organization. However, by the very nature of their jobs, the chiefs do not allow the middle to become frozen.

Chiefs in the Coast Guard, on average, have sixteen years of experience; junior officers, only two or three years. And yet, a twenty-two-year-old officer right out of the Academy outranks a thirty-six-year-old chief who has much more experience and knowledge. When a problem arises, as it sometimes does, a chief will try to solve it. If, for instance, a new officer on board a mid-sized cutter is causing some consternation among the crew, the chief will prod the ensign or the junior officer. The chief will also carry the complaint wherever it needs to go to get some action. That's the way things work all around the Coast Guard, all across the country. As one command master chief relates:

Chiefs in the Coast Guard are not afraid to kick and scream until somebody sits up and takes notice. That's one reason we're here, to look after our guys and the service as a whole. If things get broken, we do the yelling. And we know that whatever happens, we're still coming to work the next day. It's part of our job, part of our responsibility. And it's kind of like exercising your right to free speech. If something's not right, as a good citizen, you have to stand up and say something about it. So long as we're reasonable, the organization supports our actions.

The top executives in the Coast Guard, the admirals and the senior captains, clearly understand the fundamental value the chiefs provide. To a very large degree, in the Coast Guard it is acceptable to say no to your superior, as long as there is a basis in fact and truth behind the dissent. Moreover, there is a fundamental reason why such discussion and dissent is not only allowed, but encouraged. Every commissioned officer is subject to an "up or out" policy. In other words, either they are promoted during a certain time or they have to retire and leave the service. Also, they are stationed in one place for only two to four years before they receive a new assignment.

These policies, in and of themselves, help to melt the frozen layer of middle management because they keep the lower level officers on the move. If the officers want to be promoted, they have to be efficient and effective in their new positions, and they have only a certain amount of time to get things done. While there, they are forced into a sense of urgency. And more often than not, the younger officers will encourage chiefs to speak up because the chiefs have the experience and know-how to get things done.

To facilitate that process, every Coast Guard group has a command master chief who reports directly to the commanding officer, mainly to provide guidance, advice, and unfiltered communication. According to one CO, "a good command master chief knocks down barriers and connects people with needs and solutions. He's also the leader of all the other chiefs on the base, and his job is to keep them agitating and questioning. A good command master chief will always ask the question 'Why?' and a good officer will always be ready with an answer."

A frozen middle can be a real detriment to any organization. Among other things, it inhibits growth, innovation, and achievement; can actually stop change dead in its tracks; facilitates waste and running in place; and allows obstructions to build and bad feelings to fester.

The chiefs are trained to keep things moving and especially to look for obstructions that might prevent achievement. If a purchasing officer, for instance, is holding up distribution of crucial supplies by following inane federal regulations to the letter, that officer will get the business from master chiefs, senior chiefs, and warrant officers. And they will not relent until the process is flowing smoothly again and the job is getting done.

"Coast Guard chiefs are like white blood cells clustering around a disease in the human body," relates the commandant of cadets at the Coast Guard Academy. "They don't stop until the body is cured. In a very real sense, they are absolutely critical to the health and well-being of the organization."

———

After graduating from the Coast Guard Academy in 1977, newly commissioned Ensign O went straight to Portsmouth, Virginia, where he was assigned to the 327-foot, high-endurance USCGC *Ingham*. He was first assigned duty as the weapons officer (a division of the Deck Department) with a staff of six. But after only one year, he was given the position of leader of the entire Deck Department, with a staff of more than thirty-five people. Now he was responsible for the care and maintenance of the entire outside of the ship, as well as small boat maneuvers and towing operations.

"I was only twenty-three years old," he recalls. "I knew how to drive the ship, but when it came to towing boats, lowering the small boats for boarding, and other basic operations, I had no clue. They had taught us at the Academy, though, that the chiefs were the technical experts of the Coast Guard and were excellent sources of information and guidance. As officers, we were senior to them, but not superior. It was to our advantage to treat them with respect and establish professional relationships with them. So that's what I did."

On his first day, upon being assigned by the captain of the ship to commence towing operations for a stranded vessel, the young ensign immediately went to his chief petty officer, a man with seventeen years of experience in the Coast Guard. Sensing the ensign's apprehension, the chief offered his help.

"Okay, Mr. O," he said. "Here's what we're going to do. My job is to take care of you and do the right thing. I'll help you learn. You do the paperwork to start with, watch the maneuvers, and I'll take care of everything else."

Ensign O was in charge, he was personally responsible, and he had the rank. But when the boats were lowered and the towing began, he stood aside and observed as the chief ran a flawless operation.

Twenty-five years later, as a senior captain, Mr. O remembered that particular chief. "He had more of an impact on my leadership style than any other single person in the Coast Guard. I'm so glad I went to him and listened. And I really appreciate how he took me under his wing and helped me learn. I'll never forget that."

The Coast Guard on Leadership

Eliminate the Frozen Middle

- The larger the organization, the more iced up its frozen middle will be.
- Create an environment where people are not afraid to kick and scream until somebody sits up and takes notice.
- If something's not right, good citizens should speak up.
- In your organization, it should be acceptable to say no to your superiors as long as the dissent has a basis in fact and truth.
- For every satellite office, create a position that has responsibility for knocking down barriers and connecting people with needs and solutions. Have that position report directly to the executive-in-charge.
- Encourage people to ask the question "Why?" and always be ready with an answer.
- The frozen middle in any organization inhibits growth, innovation, and achievement; can actually stop change dead in its tracks; facilitates waste and running in place; and allows obstructions to build and bad feelings to fester.
- Encourage middle managers to search for obstructions that might prevent achievement. Have them work on the obstruction until the process is flowing again and the job is getting done.

Chapter 6

Cultivating Caring Relationships

The captain takes care of the crew, and
the crew takes care of the captain.

—Coast Guard maxim

Everything in leadership comes back to relationships.

"God, family, country," the captain of the air station always said to a new individual transferring in under his command. "These are my priorities in life. Sounds trite, but it's true. I'll be a man of integrity, somebody you can trust and believe in, and I'll always be trying to do the right thing. I've always put my family above my career. If you come to me and ask for advice, I'll tell you the same thing. Does that mean that I'm not going to ask you to work twenty hours in one day, or that I'm not going to call you in on weekends? No. It means that I'm going to be there for you. We're going to be there for you. We're a family. Our first mission at this air station is to take care of each other, because if we don't take care of each other, we're no good to anybody else. Remember, to command is to serve, nothing more, nothing less."

Everybody knew that this particular captain would call all hands together and tell everybody what was going on, whether there was good or bad news to report. So there was some concern when, early one morning in October 2002, he unexpectedly called a group meeting. "I'm sorry to have tell you all that the two-year-old son of one of our third-class petty officers died last night. He choked to death. Mike and his wife are going through an awfully tough time right now, as you can well imagine. In a situation like this, many people might tend to go in a different direction when they see him coming. Well, I want you to do something different. When you see Mike, whether you know him or not, I want you to go up and give him a hug. Tell him you heard about what happened and that you love him. I'm going to do all I can. But you guys please do that for him. That's how you can help."

Two weeks later, Mike asked to meet privately with the captain. "I just wanted to thank you for what you've done, Captain," he said. "I came up here about a year ago, and I wasn't sure if I wanted to stay in the Coast Guard. I was at a small boat station where the guy in charge didn't really seem to care about us. And that rubbed off on others, so that nobody ever seemed to care about anything.

"But then I came here. Everybody cared about me and about what we were doing as a unit." There was a long pause, and Mike began to cry. "And when my son died, I can't believe how people came out of the woodwork. Grown men I'd never even met before came right up to me and hugged me, cried with me, said they loved me. And you, sir. You came over to my house. You had words of comfort. You did the memorial service."

Mike broke down, sobbing. He just couldn't get any more words out. Then the captain got up from his chair, sat down on the couch next to Mike, put his arm around him, and they cried together.

God, family, country.

Back in the late 1960s, during the height of the Vietnam War, morale was generally very low in the armed forces of the United States. There were draft riots, forced conscriptions, and verbal abuse of the military.

Most of the American public did not seem to support the war. Each of the five military services earnestly studied the situation and searched for ways to improve. The U.S. Senate and House of Representatives convened hearings on the subject. As a result, Congress created the position of senior enlisted advisor for each service. The five new positions were sergeant major of the Army, master chief petty officer of the Navy, chief master sergeant of the Air Force, sergeant major of the Marine Corps, and Master Chief Petty Officer (MCPO) of the Coast Guard. Each is a staff position that reports directly to the top-level executives.

In the Coast Guard's case, the MCPO answers directly to the Commandant of the Coast Guard. At headquarters, their offices are located close to each other. The MCPO is responsible for keeping tabs on the pulse of 80 percent (the enlisted ranks) of the organization. The position is also regarded as the leader of all chiefs in the Coast Guard. When an individual is promoted to the rank of chief, the MCPO will send out a letter of congratulations and advice. "Take care of your people," the new chief will be advised. "Never forget where you came from. Teach our traditions. Be the example. Set the pace. Follow the standards of conduct."

To further expand the idea of senior enlisted advisors, the Coast Guard created the position of command master chief (CMC) and placed one in each of its major commands. One of the CMC's main roles is to be available when people in the enlisted ranks have questions. When someone asks, "Why am I performing this job?" or "Could someone please explain to me this new benefit?", the CMC provides the answers. The CMCs are the people on the team who track morale, who are specifically designated to care. If someone needs a doctor, a dentist, a chaplain, or a second chance, the CMC will get involved, make arrangements, and see things through.

In general, senior enlisted advisors are part of a much broader process in the Coast Guard that focuses specifically and strategically on building relationships and caring about people. Why? Because caring relationships are the key ingredients with which teams are built. And if the relationships among members are strong, teams are far more cohesive, efficient, and effective.

"The captain takes care of the crew, and the crew takes care of the captain" is a Coast Guard maxim that has been passed down through more than two hundred years of history and tradition. It refers to a belief that, on every deployed Coast Guard cutter, the crew interact with each other down to the basic levels of life: friendship, family, and decent human relations. As the skipper of one mid-sized cutter explains, "Out of every ten people in the Coast Guard, nine and a half are trying to take care of their shipmates to the best of their ability. It's one of our real strengths as an organization. We know if someone's grandmother has passed away, if a baby is due in the near future, or if someone just plain has the blues. We keep tabs on each other, try to lift each other's spirits, and we share experiences in both good times and bad. It makes all the difference in the world when it comes to getting the job done. We become a family, a team, not just a group of individuals thrown together."

People who are perceived *not* to care about others, or the job they are performing, or the Coast Guard's mission in general, are routinely given all sorts of attention. They are asked: "Is there a problem?" "Are you all right?" "Is something bothering you?" Almost always, the reason someone appears not to care has something to do with a personal problem. Once the problem has been identified and eliminated, the team gets back to normal.

There is not usually a deep-seated "caring" problem among Coasties because a compassionate nature is one of the characteristics for which they are selected in the first place. Why else would the crew of the USCGC *Jarvis* risk their lives to help others in need while off duty? The group had gone on a hike during a stop on the Hawaiian island of Oahu and witnessed a landslide that subsequently killed eight people and injured many more. Without a second thought, they all immediately descended into the area and, with rocks and mud falling all around them, dug out people buried in the mud, pulled the wounded to safety, and then took the time to comfort frightened children.

People generally don't enlist in the Coast Guard unless they care. The humanitarian mission itself attracts them in the first place. They know, for instance, that if they're on a cutter based on the West Coast, they may be patrolling the rookeries (breeding grounds) and haul-out areas of Steller sea lions from northern California to Alaska to enforce the Marine Mammal Protection and Endangered Species Acts. And if they're on a helicopter crew in Florida, they may be flying into the eye of a hurricane to rescue a man stuck in a tree, an elderly woman who has taken refuge on the roof of her house, or heart attack victims who can't be reached by ambulance.

Nurturing caring relationships within an organization elevates that dimension of life to a higher level. It tends to infuse compassion into everything people do, whether work-related or not. In the Coast Guard especially, there is a direct link between a caring and compassionate work force and performing caring and compassionate work with excellence. Moreover, the efforts of the work force are not limited to Coast Guard team members alone. They apply to all communities of which the organization is a part.

Even though Coast Guard personnel are weighed down with more than one job, they still find time to contribute locally by participating in volunteer fire departments and the like. As a matter of fact, all districts in the Coast Guard have a formal morale committee composed of volunteers. Any person, of any rank, may be a member. And usually it is the younger, lower ranking Coasties who become chairpersons with higher ranking personnel serving in a secondary capacity. In Juneau, Alaska, for example, the committee helps the elderly in their homes, provides meals on wheels, sponsors reading programs at local schools, supports the Boys and Girls Clubs of Juneau, purchases and distributes blankets and jackets for people who need them, and sponsors a charity fishing derby.

Being a good neighbor and helping out in your own community makes both the people being helped and those doing the helping feel good. It not only makes clients and customers feel good about the organization, it keeps internal morale high. It is precisely for these reasons that the Coast Guard sponsors morale committees all across the nation, and funds their projects with money from all goods sold at the unit exchanges.

The truth is that everything in leadership comes back to relationships. The best leaders get things done through teamwork, with teams woven together by close friendships or familylike bonds. And people never want to let down their friends and family.

Overall, an organization receives at least five major benefits when it actively cultivates caring relationships:

1. People become more fulfilled in their jobs and happier in their work.
2. People feel good about the organization.
3. Morale is kept at a high level.

4. Retention levels improve.
5. People are motivated and inspired to perform above and beyond the call of duty.

In the mid-1990s, a Coast Guard cutter based in San Juan, Puerto Rico, was on a routine reconnaissance mission in the Mona Passage between Puerto Rico and the Dominican Republic when a call came in. A mass migration of Cubans had occurred. They were ordered to proceed immediately to the Straits of Florida. The cutter ran maximum speed day and night, north up through the Mona Passage on the western coast of Puerto Rico, then west along the northern coast of the Dominican Republic and the southern coasts of the Bahamas.

When the cutter reached the Straits of Florida about noon the next day, it encountered thousands of rafts as far as the eye could see. Each raft had between twelve and twenty people on it. "It was an amazing sight," remembered the skipper of the cutter, "a huge desperate mass of humanity searching for a better way of life, risking their lives to obtain freedom. The entire crew worked tirelessly to help them."

More than a dozen other Coast Guard cutters were already there, working in rough seas. The orders were simple and straightforward: "Pick up as many people as you can." So the cutter crew began working the rafts with their standard procedure. Bring the raft alongside. Embark the emigrants. Organize them in an orderly way on the boat. Set up a check station. Conduct a medical check. Give everybody some water. Give them a blue pad to sit on. Give them a blanket. Give them an identification tag. If they're healthy enough, process their paperwork. If not, tend to their medical needs.

One raft had seventeen adults and one child on it. All were severely dehydrated, some had their eyes rolled back in their heads and were convulsing. One member of the crew, a seaman second-class named Tim, spent the entire day tending to these victims. He gave them food, water, medical help. In the end, they all survived.

By the time the crew of the cutter quit at two o'clock in the morning, they had worked 42 rafts and had taken 345 people on board. Then the Coast Guard cutter sailed directly to the Naval Station at Guantanamo Bay, Cuba, and delivered all the Cuban emigrants to safety.

THE COAST GUARD ON LEADERSHIP

Cultivate Caring Relationships

- Create a position similar to a "senior enlisted advisor" for the purpose of keeping tabs on the pulse of the ranks of the organization who are not upper management. Have that position report directly to the chief executive officer.
- Also create a position equivalent to a command master chief in each satellite office of the organization with the same responsibility as the senior enlisted advisor.
- Caring relationships are the key ingredients by which cohesive, efficient, and effective teams are built.
- Nurturing caring relationships within an organization elevates that dimension of life to a higher level. It tends to infuse compassion into everything people do, whether work-related or not.
- Create a morale committee dedicated to being a good neighbor and helping out the local community. It will make customers and clients feel good about the organization and will keep internal morale high.
- Leaders get things done through teamwork—and the best teams are woven together with relationships that are more like close friendships and families than anything else.
- There are five major benefits to an organization that cultivates caring relationships:
  1. People become more fulfilled in their jobs and happier in the work they do
  2. People feel good about the organization
  3. Morale stays at a high level
  4. Retention levels improve
  5. People are motivated and inspired to perform above and beyond the call of duty.

Chapter 7

Build Strong Alliances

In any given year, the Coast Guard Auxiliary volunteers more than
2 million hours, saves more than 300 lives, participates in
36,000 operational support missions, educates tens of
thousands of people on boating safety, and is
credited with providing approximately $1
billion in service to the United States.
That is the power of a well
organized, formal alliance
with people who care.

On 11 December 1941, only four days after the Japanese bombed Pearl
Harbor, Germany declared war on the United States. The next day, Adolf
Hitler met with the head of the German Navy and gave an order to deploy
submarines off the Atlantic coast of the United States. The first German
subs appeared off Massachusetts in January 1942. By late April, many of
these submarines were inflicting considerable damage off the coast of
Florida. In May the *New York Times* reported that more than one hundred
fifty ships had been sunk in the Atlantic by these enemy submarines.

U.S. Coast Guard Auxiliary flotillas in Florida quickly organized themselves all along the coastline. They responded when an oil tanker was torpedoed and sunk about five miles off Cape Canaveral, rescuing survivors and picking up bodies. And they steadfastly maintained regular patrols up and down the coast in order to keep a lookout, so they could be the eyes and ears of the Coast Guard.

Late one night, Captain Williard Lewis (known in the region as "Old Williard") was out by himself near the Hillsboro Lighthouse off Fort Lauderdale. Suddenly, he heard a loud movement of water and turned to see the silhouette of a German submarine against the night sky. He immediately radioed the Coast Guard about the surfacing, but, while waiting, he became increasingly worried that they might not arrive in time. So Old Williard decided that he would take matters into his own hands and ram the submarine with his 32-foot cabin cruiser.

As he steamed toward the German U-boat, a sailor popped out of the conning tower of the sub and ran down toward the 50-caliber deck gun. Then a siren sounded, the German ran back inside, and the submarine turned and headed out to sea. Old Willard chased the sub for about a mile until it finally submerged.

By late May, German U-boats had headed into the Gulf of Mexico. They were met by patrolling members of the Coast Guard Auxiliary, several of whom had actually chased off a submarine trying to head up the Mississippi River. Unable to make any headway in the gulf, the Germans finally abandoned their mission and left the southeastern and southern coasts of the United States.

In the 1930s a tragic boating accident occurred off the coast of California in which a life was lost and, due to the remote location, the Coast Guard was unable to respond. Within a couple of days, local civilian boaters contacted their friends at the Coast Guard and requested a meeting to discuss the matter. The two groups already had a good relationship going. They had been informally working together for decades. But now, in the wake of this particular accident, and in view of increased boating activity along the coast, the civilians suggested the creation of a new, more formal alliance. "[It] would be an excellent thing," they suggested, "to place at the disposal of Coast Guard officers, auxiliary flotillas of small craft for the frequent emergencies incident to your duties."

Subsequently, in 1939, the Coast Guard Reserve, a group of volunteers, was created. Two years later, at the onset of World War II, Congress restructured the Reserve to function as a source of military manpower, like the present-day reserves of the armed services. In peacetime, its mission would be to provide extra port and homeland security when necessary. The existing civilian organization was then renamed the Coast Guard Auxiliary.

Initially, the Auxiliary taught boating safety education to the public. Its mission was viewed as "preventive search and rescue." The reasoning was sound: If boaters were taught how to be safe on the water, there would be fewer people needing to be rescued by the Coast Guard. The Auxiliary, with its own boats, also began patrolling waters whenever and wherever it could. And during the four years of World War II, it became the eyes and ears of the Coast Guard: a dedicated civilian force on guard across the nation, watching out for threats to homeland security.

By creating this formal alliance with American citizens, the Coast Guard increased its reach and became more effective at performing its missions. Coast Guard leaders were not afraid to step out of their own organization to work with outsiders in a team environment. But that was nothing new. It's one of the organization's secrets to success, one of the ways it is able to achieve so many missions with so few people.

The Coast Guard has formal alliances with dozens of organizations throughout the nation. The Civil Air Patrol, for instance, regularly supplements SAR cases with its civilian-owned and -operated aircraft. The U.S. Army Corps of Engineers is another good example. Both organizations are highly focused on the nation's inland waterways, and there are many places where their work is very similar. So they work hand in hand on numerous projects across the country. The Coast Guard also works closely with the National Marine Fisheries Office on regulation and enforcement of fisheries management. A Vessel Location System (VLS) transponder is required on all fishing vessels operating in U.S. fisheries. Using global positioning technology, the National Marine Fisheries Office monitors the fishing boats. If one crosses into an area where the waters have been significantly overfished, or into an area that is closed, the Coast Guard is called in to enforce the law. Such violations often result in fines of between $25,000 and $100,000. Severe cases result in licenses being revoked. By working together in this formal alliance, both organizations are able to better fulfill their missions.

The same is true of the Coast Guard relationship with the U.S. Navy. In past wars, the Coast Guard actually became a division of the Navy. In peacetime, the two maritime military services work together closely in a variety of venues. For instance, under a national fleet policy concept, they work together in areas ranging from acquisition, maintenance, and modernization programs to joint mission operations. There is also a formally constituted Navy/Coast Guard board that meets twice each year (or more often, if needed) to press forward on a common agenda.

In addition, the Coast Guard optimizes its role as a regulator and facilitator of the marine industry by forging both formal and informal alliances with trade associations involved in the maritime trade. The American Waterways Operators (AWO), for example, linked forces with the Coast Guard to establish goals and standards in the industry. As a result, maritime operations are safer and more efficient.

With the Auxiliary, however, the Coast Guard created the ultimate alliance. It essentially enlisted the aid of American citizens nationwide who were willing to help their country. More than that, though, the Auxiliary was made a formal member of the Coast Guard team in virtually every sense of the word.

At the turn of the twenty-first century, the Coast Guard Auxiliary had more than thirty-three thousand members located in all fifty states, Puerto Rico, the Virgin Islands, American Samoa, and Guam. To join, people must be U.S. citizens, at least seventeen years of age, and must have at least a quarter-interest in a boat, aircraft, radio station, or have skills of value to the Coast Guard. The average age of an auxiliarist is fifty. They represent nearly every vocation and avocation you can think of, from truck drivers to corporate vice presidents, from Ph.D.s to people with high school educations, from accountants to plumbers, from computer technicians to carpet layers. They are close-knit teams of volunteers who teach public safety on Tuesday nights, have flotilla meetings on Thursday nights, and patrol in their boats on Fridays and Saturdays.

The official purpose of the Coast Guard Auxiliary is "to assist the Coast Guard, as authorized by the Commandant, in performing any Coast Guard function, power, duty, role, mission, or operation authorized by law."

Specifically, auxiliarists assist the Coast Guard in non–law enforcement programs, such as vessel safety checks, safety patrols, search and rescue, and marine environmental protection. They participate in nearly every Coast Guard mission, with the exception of military or law enforcement operations. They utilize more than five thousand of their own vessels, several hundred of their own aircraft, and several thousand private communications facilities. While the U.S. Coast Guard, under federal statute, is responsible for educating the public on boating safety, no active duty member does so. That responsibility is delegated to the Auxiliary.

In any given year, the Coast Guard Auxiliary volunteers give more than two million hours, save more than three hundred lives, participate in thirty-six thousand operational support missions, and educate tens of thousands of people on boating safety. Moreover, the Auxiliary is credited with providing approximately $1 billion in service to the United States. And in a national emergency, the Coast Guard can literally double its number of members by deploying the Auxiliary. That is the power of a well-organized formal alliance with people who care.

In leadership, strong alliances offer four key benefits:

1. They leverage and multiply productivity and results for both organizations.
2. They expand contacts and networks of communication.
3. They strengthen forces and shore up weaknesses.
4. They help individuals gain more energy and enthusiasm.

Building strong alliances, however, does not come naturally to many executives in large organizations. And that is especially the case when it comes to partnerships with retired people or others who might be willing to volunteer their time. Resistance by managers is often due to fear of competition and feeling threatened that somebody with more experience will perform better. "No, no, we have our own people who do those jobs," a typical reply might be. "We don't need volunteers doing them, or anybody else, for that matter."

When the suggestion was made to use volunteers back in the 1930s, leaders in the Coast Guard gave exactly the opposite response. "That's not a bad idea," they said. "Older citizens with broad, diversified experience, with knowledge of the sea, boating, and all kinds of other varied expertise, could really help us get a lot accomplished."

After the Coast Guard embraced the civilians who make up the Auxiliary, brought them into the organization, offered them training, showed their appreciation, and made everybody proud to be part of the Coast Guard, what did it receive in return? The Coast Guard got a major resource filled with people who work long hours in the performance of their duties, who love, respect, and are devoted to the Coast Guard. And who do not receive a salary for their efforts; they are all volunteers.

Why do the members of the Coast Guard Auxiliary donate their time, energy, and skills? They do so for the same reasons most people will say they want to be involved: because they want to feel a part of something bigger than themselves, because they want to do something valuable, because they want to contribute, and most important, because they care.

The great World War II hero and aviator, General Jimmy Doolittle, said it best: "There is nothing like the heart of a volunteer."

At 4:30 in the afternoon, on Monday, 21 January 2000, the Channel Islands Coast Guard station in Oxnard, California, received an emergency call from the crew of a local fishing vessel. There had been a large splash at sea, they reported, and it had gone about 200 feet into the air!

The chief petty officer in charge of the small boat station immediately dispatched two 40-foot motor lifeboats and ordered that the Auxiliary be contacted. Moments later, a commodore in the local Coast Guard Auxiliary (who also happened to be chairman of the board of a large tool company) received the word on his cellular phone while driving home from the office. He quickly scrambled the half-dozen members of his crew (five men and one woman, with an average age of seventy), and within minutes they were all headed out to sea on board *Mr. Chips VI,* the commodore's 60-foot Hatteras sports fisher. Meanwhile, a park ranger had called in and reported seeing a commercial jet liner go down. And the FAA had reported that Alaska Airlines flight 87, flying from Mexico to Seattle with eighty-eight people on board, had disappeared from the radar screen.

When *Mr. Chips VI* arrived on scene to join the two small Coast Guard boats, the seas were rough and darkness was closing in fast. All kinds of debris were floating on the water: pieces of airplane, luggage with Alaska

Airlines tags, jet fuel, body parts. The chief petty officer ordered a full-scale search and rescue operation; over the next hour or so, many helicopters and boats swarmed over the scene. In the interim, the crew of Mr. Chips VI began cruising back and forth among the debris, searching for survivors, pulling various materials out of the water. They continued doing so well into the night.

Over the next several days, Mr. Chips VI shuttled FBI agents and other investigators back and forth. They took ministers out to counsel people who were dealing with the recovery of body parts. While all active Coast Guard personnel were on the scene of the accident, other members of the Auxiliary flooded into the station to handle normal day-to-day operations, such as answering the phones, taking care of reports and other paperwork, and handling 911 calls at sea. Finally, as no survivors were encountered, the entire operation was shifted from search and rescue to search and recovery, at which point the Navy took over formal control from the Coast Guard.

On the one-year anniversary of the crash, members of the local Coast Guard Auxiliary, led by the crew of Mr. Chips VI, coordinated memorial services both on the beach and on the water for several hundred family members of the victims. They were joined by dozens of other private boats and thousands of private citizens. As the chief petty officer originally in charge of the operation stated: "Our Auxiliary demonstrated the finest qualities of America in action."

THE COAST GUARD ON LEADERSHIP

Build Strong Alliances

- Don't be afraid to step out of your own organization to work with outsiders in a team environment.
- Create formal alliances with dozens of groups. It's one of the secrets to organizational success.
- In the case of the best groups, take the alliance one step further and make them a formal part of your organization.
- Don't be afraid to delegate some responsibility to those groups with whom you form alliances.
- There are four main benefits to building strong alliances:
    1. They leverage and multiply productivity and results
    2. They expand contacts and networks of communication
    3. They strengthen forces and shore up weaknesses
    4. They help individuals gain more energy and enthusiasm.
- Many people in large organizations resist forming alliances with retired people or volunteers.
- When you show your appreciation to people and make them proud to be part of your organization, they will work long hours in the performance of their duties and will be devoted to the organization.
- Recall the words of Gen. Jimmy Doolittle: "There's nothing like the heart of a volunteer."

Chapter 8

Create an Effective
Communication System

At least once a month, I get [the officers] together whether they like it or
not. And I tell them to take off their shoulder boards when they attend
CO meetings. We're there to hear each other out, bring up
problem issues, and solve them as a team. The only way
we can really do that is to talk honestly and openly
with each other—as people, not as one officer
reporting to a higher ranking officer. And
once we've arrived at a decision, everybody
has to support our course of action.
We must have one collective
voice when we exit.

—Coast Guard commanding officer, Kodiak, Alaska

What is said in the Chiefs' Mess <u>stays</u> in the Chiefs' Mess.

—Coast Guard adage

One day in 2001, the USCGC *Munro*, a 378-foot, high-endurance cutter based in Alameda, California, was performing drug interdiction patrols off the coast of Panama in a joint effort with the U.S. Navy. The 175-person crew had been out to sea for fifty days without touching or seeing land. They were tired, homesick, and looking forward to going back to California in only three days.

But early that afternoon the skipper of the *Munro* received a dispatch from the Joint Interagency Task Force (JIATF) out of Key West, Florida. An emergency had come up. The Navy had received intelligence that a series of drug runs was about to take place. They were short on ships, so the *Munro* was ordered to extend duty another thirty days. Immediately, the captain summoned all nine officers to the wardroom for a briefing. Then he held a private meeting with the command master chief, passed on the information, and expressed concern for the crew's morale.

"Don't worry, sir," replied the master chief, "the crew will be fine. We'll take care of everything."

A few minutes later, an announcement went out over the ship's speaker system: "Chiefs' call in ten minutes. Chiefs' call in ten minutes."

All fourteen chief petty officers dropped what they were doing and quickly gathered in the chiefs' mess. At first, there was stunned silence at the news. Then there were a number of four-letter words shouted, along with other colorful expletives. Several of the chiefs continued to voice their disapproval.

"Okay, okay," said one of the senior chiefs. "We've got a problem here."

"Yeah, if we're not careful, morale will go all to hell," said another. "Well, how do you want to handle it?"

"Shall we tell them all together or tell them by department?"

"Let's meet with them in our own groups. It'll be more personal that way."

"I agree. That way, they'll feel more comfortable yelling. Then they can get it all out of their system."

"Okay, what do we tell them?"

"We tell them the truth. We tell them everything. And after they get all the bellyaching out of their systems, we compliment them. Tell them they've been doing a great job. Remind them of our mission in the Coast Guard, that we're on duty for our country. And tell them that we're proud to be serving with them. That we're proud to be on the same team with them. That they're the best."

"Does everybody concur?" asked the command master chief.

Heads nodded all around.

"Okay, then. Let's get to it."

Small meetings were then held all over the ship, in the engine room, on the deck, in the galley, anywhere the chiefs could get some privacy with their people. Within an hour from the time the dispatch was first received from JIATF, every member of the *Munro*'s crew knew the score. Later that afternoon, all hands met on the helicopter pad for quarters. The captain reaffirmed the new orders and thanked everybody for understanding. Although many of the crew members were displeased and disappointed, they didn't show it. They went on to serve a total of more than eighty days at sea and concluded their mission with pride.

G reat leaders know the value of effective communication. They understand that when their organizations communicate well, they are better able to eliminate "stovepipes" and fiefdoms, build trust, foster relationships, mobilize teams, and, in so doing, achieve success.

Because their missions are crucial to the health and well-being of the United States and its citizens, leaders in the Coast Guard have put in place a system of communication so consistent, so ongoing, and so meaningful that it is difficult to imagine how any organization could do a better job. And it all begins at the top.

The Commandant of the Coast Guard surrounds himself with a close-knit group of trusted advisors who willingly work together in a team. Then he listens to them and involves them in decision making. One of those advisors is the Master Chief Petty Officer of the Coast Guard, who is designated as an unfiltered line of communication to the Commandant, to whom the position reports directly. The MCPO pays attention to everybody— officers, civilians, contractors, family members, and so forth—because they all affect the enlisted ranks that make up 80 percent of the organization.

Anyone and everyone is able to call, write, send e-mail, or have personal contact with the MCPO to discuss any issue of concern to them: pay, unfair treatment, concern about general direction or strategy, anything.

The relationship between the Commandant and the MCPO is then replicated throughout the Coast Guard. Gold-badge master chiefs report directly to three-star admirals in the field for the same purpose. Silver-badge master chiefs report to two-star admirals. And in every major Coast Guard command, there are command master chiefs who report directly to the commanding officer (CO). In turn, each CO (usually a captain) holds regular meetings with the officer corps. As one captain explains it: "At least once a month, I get them all together whether they like it or not. And I tell them to take off their shoulder boards [which designate rank] when they attend CO meetings. We're there to hear each other out, bring up problem issues, and solve them as a team. They only way we can really do that is to talk honestly and openly with each other as people, not as one officer reporting to a higher ranking officer. And once we've arrived at a decision, everybody has to support our course of action. We must have one collective voice when we exit."

Most COs will hold a monthly meeting with all hands. "I want everybody to know what the group has accomplished that month," states another captain. "A lot of the guys are in the shops fixing an engine, or someplace similar. I want them to know why they're doing it. I want to tell them what's coming up. And I want to recognize top performance. That's why we present awards and single out individual and group achievements at every monthly all hands meeting."

Wise commanding officers also meet regularly with their chief petty officers. Some have breakfast with the chiefs, tell them what's going on, ask what's on their minds, ask what they might need from the CO. Gatherings like this are all about meeting with people face to face rather than sending them e-mail or memoranda. Leaders in the Coast Guard realize that personal human contact is the most important and effective form of communication available to them.

No group practices that concept better than the chiefs who, as middle-level leaders, are the action part of the organization. Their job is to get things done. They do so, principally, through nearly perfect teamwork. On every cutter, for instance, and in every onshore location, there is a chiefs' mess, a special place where the chief petty officers meet to discuss ongoing activity. The chiefs hang out there during breaks in activity. There may be only a few present at any given time. But regularly, usually once a month on land and once a week on board ship, a more formal "chiefs' call" will be held. Normal operations are discussed at these meetings. If there is a better way to accomplish the mission, the chiefs want to discuss it. In addition, whenever an emergency comes up, one that demands quick action, a chiefs' call is immediately convened.

Any chief may call such a meeting. It may be held in the chiefs' mess, at a restaurant, in somebody's garage, or in any other place where the chiefs can talk among themselves. After the issue has been discussed and debated, a plan of action is determined and agreed upon. If people disagree, they are allowed to say why, to express their emotions and get it off their chest so that everything is out in the open. But the chiefs also have an adage they live by: "What is said in the chiefs' mess stays in the chiefs' mess." Nothing anyone says in a chiefs' call will ever be held against them. The main idea is for everybody to leave the mess with a unified voice. They do not want open complaining from a member of the group who disagrees. It doesn't look good, it's not good for morale, and it almost always harms implementation and achievement of the mission.

The officers' equivalent of the chiefs' mess is called the wardroom. This is where officers meet on a regular basis and perform functions similar to those of the chiefs, but more specific to their particular duties. Every evening on board ship, for example, officers meet in the wardroom to discuss the next day's agenda. Then the executive officer (XO) formally writes up a new plan of the day (POD) that is posted on the wall and on electronic bulletin boards. The next day, an all-hands meeting, termed quarters, is held.

When in port, quarters is usually held twice a week. When the ship is under way, it's held every day (except Sundays), usually around twelve thirty. Just before every quarters, the chiefs often meet in the wardroom with the officers to make certain that everybody passes the same messages along to the crew. Then the entire ship's company gathers. On a 378-foot, high-endurance cutter, for instance, everybody lines up in formation on the helicopter pad. Awards and/or citations are read by the XO and presented by the captain. After that, the captain will say, "Okay, everybody, gather 'round." The crew then crowds around the captain and the XO in an informal atmosphere. The XO begins by reviewing important parts of the plan of the day, and any other items that have come up since the plan was posted. At this point, new people are introduced to the crew and people being transferred out are invited to say goodbye. Then everybody breaks up into four different groups by ship's department—Engineering, Supply, Weapons, and Operations—where they receive more detailed briefings by the department heads.

Quarters is held for several important reasons. First, it ensures that everybody is present and on duty. Second, it transmits important information to everybody all at once on a regular basis. In this way directives from the Commandant of the Coast Guard are relayed directly to Coasties on the deck plate. Third, because quarters provides information personally, it ensures true accountability. No one can say they have not gotten the word. Not only is the plan of the day posted, it is discussed in person with every member of the crew present and also in teams, by department. Fourth, it provides a forum where people are recognized by their peers, both formally and informally. Fifth, it provides an opportunity, on a frequent and regular basis, for the captain (the chief executive) to address the crew and for the crew to interact with the captain.

An effective system of communication is important in the Coast Guard for the same reason it's important in leadership. For one thing, it gets everybody on the same page. That increases the probability of mission accomplishment. In addition, every good leader knows that not having accurate, up-to-date information can kill any chances of achieving the organization's mission. But the very best leaders also intuitively understand that a lack of good relationships can be as fatal as a lack of critical information.

Relationships are built on mutual respect and trust. But respect and trust can only be earned through constant, ongoing, dynamic communication. It is from that type of communication that relationships grow. And once again, everything in leadership comes back to relationships.

THE COAST GUARD ON LEADERSHIP

Create an Effective Communication System

- An effective system of communication eliminates "stovepipes" and fiefdoms, builds trust, fosters relationships, mobilizes teams, and, in so doing, achieves success.
- Surround the chief executive of the organization with a close-knit group of trusted advisors who willingly work together in a team.
- Replicate that close-knit group of advisors for every leading executive in every location in the organization.
- Hold regular meetings with your immediate team, in which you talk to each other honestly and openly without reference to position or rank.
- Hold an all-hands meeting at least once a month. Explain what's coming up and single out individual and group excellence.
- Meet regularly, perhaps at breakfast, with the middle-level leaders in the organization. Tell them what's going on, ask what's on their minds, and ask what they might need from you.
- Remember that personal human contact is the most important and effective form of communication available to you.
- Designate a special place where leaders can meet, both formally and informally, to discuss ongoing activity. Keep those discussions private. Remember: "What is said in the chiefs' mess stays in the chiefs' mess."
- Once a decision has been made, be certain that everyone presents a united front to the troops.
- During critical activities, meet every day with your team. Review plans, break up into smaller groups by department, and encourage informal discussions and updates.
- Relationships are built on mutual respect and trust. But respect and trust can only be earned through constant, ongoing, dynamic communication.

PART THREE

Instill a Bias for Action

Chapter 9

Make Change the Norm

That young man is right. This old procedure is not going to sail. Let's make the change. . . . Let's think about tomorrow.

—Coast Guard admiral, when informed of an enlisted mate's suggestion of how to be more effective

With a couple of hundred years of evolution and experience, leaders in the Coast Guard intrinsically understand the need to change. They have created, perpetuated, and are part of an organizational environment where change is fostered on a regular basis—where it is, essentially, a natural state of affairs.

An electrician's mate third-class, recently stationed on a medium-endurance cutter based in Newport, Rhode Island, saw what he thought was a problem. So he went to his chief.

"Policy says I have to go to a three-week school to learn how to repair an air conditioning unit," he said. "But wouldn't it be better just to have an extra unit on board to replace the old one? Then we could send the broken one off for repairs. That would be a lot cheaper than sending me away for three weeks to an expensive school, wouldn't it? And then I'd be here to perform my other work, too."

The chief warrant officer agreed and contacted the Engineering Support Unit at First District headquarters in Boston. "I think we have a problem," he said as he began to explain the situation.

"Good point," came the response. "We'd better take a closer look at that."

Within a few days, the Acquisitions Department at Coast Guard Headquarters in Washington, D.C., had formed a small team to look at the situation. They studied the details and ultimately came to the conclusion that the electrician's mate third-class was right. The team then formulated a plan for change and presented it to the admiral responsible for purchasing material on board ships. He listened, asked questions, discussed the issue, and finally agreed.

"That young man is right," concluded the admiral. "It's cheaper to buy an extra unit and have it on board ship than it is to send him to a training school for three weeks. This old procedure is not going to sail. Let's make the change."

Less than a month after the electrician's mate third-class had discussed the idea with his chief, people were discussing the new policy on board cutters all around the Coast Guard. And then the new procedure was implemented with a formal directive.

But action on the matter didn't end with that particular decision. "What other things are we doing that we probably should not be doing anymore?" asked the admiral. So a larger task force was formed at headquarters with the following charge: "Let's get with our ratings master chiefs and look at everything in this regard. Let's make changes where we need to. What kind of people are we going to staff? What kind of training will they receive? How many people do we need to perform each and every function? Let's think about tomorrow."

Imagine that! A working sailor in Rhode Island speaks up about what he thought was a better way to get things done, and then actually sees his idea put into practice across the entire country. Although not all suggestions result in major change, in the U.S. Coast Guard it is the norm for honest suggestions to be seriously considered. This story is also a good illustration of a rather informal but genuine approach to change that is employed routinely throughout the organization. That approach consists of the following four steps:

1. Be open-minded. Listen for better ways to get things done.
2. Involve others. Study the merits, and if the idea passes muster, create a plan with vision and goals.
3. Prepare people for the change. Explain the whole story, answer questions, make sure people understand why.
4. Implement the change with broad-based communication including written directives and personal contact.

Leadership is all about change. Leaders take people where they haven't been before. They blaze new trails, plow new ground, sail uncharted waters. Leaders themselves are agents of change. If they're not changing, they're not leading. It's that simple.

After all, change, in and of itself, is part of the natural flow of life. Technology changes, markets change, the world changes, and people change. Most business corporations that fail do so because their executives don't adapt and change with the times. They don't listen when their customers complain, react when their markets adjust, or act before they're in a serious crisis.

The Coast Guard, however, does listen, does react, and does act before a major crisis occurs. Part of the organization's culture is to constantly change, constantly adapt, constantly find ways to do things better and more efficiently. In part, the Coast Guard's missions, because of their importance, drive this need to change. The Coast Guard is, after all, a service organization dedicated to saving lives, protecting and defending the nation, and enforcing laws for the benefit of all citizens.

Looking back on a couple of hundred years of evolution and experience, leaders in the Coast Guard understand the need to change. They have created, perpetuated, and become part of an organizational environment where change is fostered on a regular basis, where it is a natural state of affairs.

All proposed changes in the Coast Guard are studied so as to gain a complete understanding of both positive and negative consequences. Sometimes, no change is made, instead existing policy is reaffirmed. Other times, policies are modified. But always, the long-term best interests of the organization are carefully evaluated, especially in individual personnel situations.

For example, all active members of the Coast Guard transfer to a new assignment every two to four years. Sometimes they stay in the same area, but most of the time, they move to a new geographic place, taking their families with them. As a result, they are constantly making changes in both their professional and personal lives. Once in a while, that creates personal problems with spouses and children who may not want to move so frequently. In such cases, there is an outlet for modification of assigned changes. But most Coast Guard families view the constant movement as normal, at least for them. It's exciting to have a new adventure every couple of years. It's exciting to see new things, meet new people, learn new cultures. So in the spring every year, all across the Coast Guard, there is a heightened sense of excitement as people anticipate their new assignments. Then, in the summer, as much as 20 percent of the work force is in transit.

As a result of this ongoing transfer process, nearly every team in the Coast Guard, whether large or small, has a range of experience levels. That, in turn, creates a learning cycle that affects almost all personnel. Early in their new assignments, they learn how to do their jobs effectively. Then, while they're performing their work, they teach and coach new people who might end up being their replacements. The whole idea is to perpetuate the function of the team, to make certain things continue to be done efficiently so that the organization's missions are achieved.

"For me, the Coast Guard is like life," says one junior officer, "with new beginnings, new relationships, new places. Always having another mountain to climb. Learning to scale that mountain with your friends. Celebrating victory together. Then sliding back down to the valley to teach new guys who come in, to give them the tools to climb a mountain of their own. There's also a time to move on. Then the whole thing starts all over again."

The Coast Guard's long-standing personnel rotation policies are frequently reviewed on a case-by-case basis so that both the best interests of the individual to be transferred and the organization as a whole are weighed fairly. Balancing traditional policy and the impact of new influences is a fundamental part the Coast Guard's organizational, unit, and personal life, and has become part of the Coast Guard's climate of change.

On balance, despite ongoing family and unit disruptions, transferring employees on a regular basis provides several major advantages for the Coast Guard:

1. It creates an action-oriented, dynamic organization where people are always "on the move."
2. It molds people into well-rounded individuals with a broader range of experience and knowledge.
3. By providing new opportunities, it eliminates boredom and complacency, and keeps people excited and energized.
4. It offers parity among job personnel because assignments eventually rotate.
5. It creates a continual learning environment and a natural way to pass on training and leadership skills.
6. It facilitates innovative ways of thinking because with new people come new ideas.
7. It keeps experience levels staggered, which, in turn, provides a more diverse range of opinions, leading to a better overall outcome.
8. It standardizes procedures across the organization.

There is one other system in the Coast Guard that facilitates change in an unusual and, some would say, unconventional manner for a major organization. All officers (who make up the upper level and part of the middle level of leadership) are subject to an "up or out" policy. In other words, they must either attain promotion within a certain time frame or else retire from the service.

On the surface, such a policy sounds a bit harsh or extreme. However, it was Coast Guard officers who implemented the system in the first place, and it provides a couple of significant benefits.

First of all, the "up or out" policy tends to breed a climate of action, focus, and constructive competition at the highest levels of an organization. As people rise through their careers, and the pyramid narrows, fewer and fewer positions become available. As a result, the people who are chosen for the highest levels of leadership tend to be the cream of the crop. They are promoted because they are action-oriented and perform their jobs with excellence.

Second, the policy benefits younger officers in that it continually creates openings for upward mobility and advancement. Ambitious young people then have something for which to strive. They know that if, over the course of their careers, they work hard and perform well, they may advance on their own merits and there will be openings to fill.

The "up or out" policy adds an interesting dimension to the ingrained process of change in the Coast Guard. And remember, leadership is all about change.

In 1972, the superintendent of the Coast Guard Academy directed the commandant of cadets to conduct a study on whether or not women should be admitted as cadets to the Coast Guard Academy. There had been quite a storm brewing over women's rights across the nation, and the superintendent felt that the Coast Guard should at least look into the feasibility of taking such a step. The study concluded that, from a technical or mechanical perspective, there was simply no basis for excluding women from the academy. In spite of this finding, enough traditionalist senior officers were opposed to the change that it was not seriously considered for implementation at that time.

By 1975, however, public opinion had heated up to such a point that Congress began considering legislation that would order all the military service academies to admit women. It was at this point that the Commandant of the Coast Guard and the chief of staff decided to "get out in front of this bow wave." They dusted off the old 1972 report, reexamined the issue, and laid it open for serious discussion.

These two men realized that the world had changed. They were visionaries who were open to new ideas, new ways of doing things. They looked beyond the old stereotypes of women that emphasized limitations, restrictions, and predetermined social roles. Still they encountered a lot of resistance from traditionalists at headquarters. The issue was debated, sometimes in a most heated manner. Emotions ran strong. Honest men lobbied strongly against having women at the academy. Everyone's voice was heard. And when all was said and done, the Coast Guard decided to admit women because it was an idea whose time had come.

In August 1975, the Commandant formally announced that women would be admitted to the Coast Guard Academy that next summer. The superintendent of the Academy was very supportive of the change. He immediately called the entire staff and faculty together. "The Coast Guard has decided that women should share equal opportunity and responsibility with men at our academy," he told them. "So we're going forward. We're going to make this work. We're not going to put up any obstacles. I want and expect full cooperation from everyone in this room."

Congress passed the bill in the fall of 1975, it was signed into law by the president of the United States, and the other military academies followed suit. Four years after that, the Coast Guard Academy, in its class of 1980, graduated fourteen women from its ranks and commissioned them ensigns in the United States Coast Guard.

Twenty years later, at the turn of the twenty-first century, one-third of the entire corps of cadets were women. Some old traditionalists, then retired, were still shaking their heads over the change.

The Coast Guard on Leadership

Make Change the Norm

- Approach change with the following four steps:
  1. Be open-minded and listen for better ways to get things done
  2. Involve others, study the merits, and if the idea passes muster, create a plan with vision and goals
  3. Prepare people for the change by explaining the whole story and answering their questions
  4. Implement the change with broad-based communication.
- Change, in and of itself, is part of the natural flow of life.
- Create an environment in your organization that fosters change on a regular basis.
- Transferring employees on a regular basis provides several major advantages to an organization:
  1. It creates an action-oriented, dynamic organization where people are always "on the move."
  2. It molds people into well-rounded individuals with broader ranges of experience and knowledge.
  3. By providing new opportunities, it eliminates boredom and complacency, and keeps people excited and energized.
  4. It offers parity among job personnel because assignments eventually rotate.
  5. It creates a continual learning environment and a natural way to pass on training and leadership skills.
  6. It facilitates new and innovative thinking because with new people come new ideas.
  7. It keeps experience levels staggered, which, in turn, provides a more diverse range of opinions.
  8. It standardizes procedures across the organization.
- An "up or out" policy tends to breed action, focus, and constructive competition at the highest levels of an organization.
- Remember that leadership is all about change.

Chapter 10

Encourage Decisiveness

In the Coast Guard, the filter between the policy-writer
and the doer is as thin as a single sheet of paper.

Do what you have to do. Act first. Call me later.

—Standing order from headquarters to a
Coast Guard leader in the field

One of the first things the Seventh District commander did upon assuming
his new position in 1999 was to go out into the field and visit the troops.
He wanted to get the lay of the land, meet the Coasties who were on the
boats, and find out what was good and what could be better.

But as the admiral traveled around the district from northern Florida to
Puerto Rico, he noticed that operational boat crews were wearing different
uniforms depending on location. And it struck him as odd. "Why would
Coasties in the Gulf wear different uniforms than Coasties in the

Caribbean?" he wondered. So he asked many of them why that was the case and what they thought about it. And the responses he received were unusually honest and revealing.

"It all depends on what the CO thinks we should be wearing," said one. "It's really kind of silly, isn't it?" commented another. "I don't see why we have to wear these full uniforms when we're out at sea," said one young woman. "It gets hot out here and we're always uncomfortable."

Upon returning to headquarters, the admiral brought up the subject at his next CO meeting. After discussing the issue and considering a variety of solutions and consequences, they decided to standardize uniforms across the district for operational boat crews and people who were out on site doing their jobs. The new uniform would consist of working pants, black boots, white socks, and tee-shirts that had "USCG" on the chest.

That decision sent shock waves throughout the rest of the district. Accountants immediately raised their hands and complained about having to buy all these new tee-shirts. "You can't buy the shirts with our general fund," they stated. "There's a requirement that prevents it. It's a rule."

Word on the decision and its resulting controversy had quickly spread throughout the Coast Guard, and everybody watched carefully to see what the outcome would be.

The Seventh District commander acknowledged to the accountants that they were, indeed, correct in stating that there was a rule against purchasing the shirts with money from the general fund. But then he did something unusual. He got the lawyers in the district together, and they changed the rule. Then he put the word out to everybody. "If there's a rule that has been in place for a long time, and it doesn't fit the operational requirements, or it's kind of stupid," he said, "then break the rule and do what you need to do to get the job done. Just make sure you can support the decision."

Decision making in leadership is all about action. Taking action, making things happen, getting the job done. Without effective decision making, any organization is ruined. People wander about aimlessly, aggressive employees become frustrated, and lethargic employees are not motivated. Worst of all, nothing gets done, except by the most action-oriented, maverick employees who would rather risk losing their jobs than sit around twiddling their thumbs.

An organization with decisive leadership, however, almost naturally creates a dynamic and vibrant atmosphere. People move about with a spring in their step and purpose in their direction. Effective decision making, when implemented properly, is a continuous, uninterrupted process similar to the beating of a heart that sends blood throughout a body. Quite literally, it pumps life into an organization.

Because of its varied and important missions, and because of its relatively small number of active duty personnel, the Coast Guard can't afford to have anybody just sitting around. Moreover, since it recruits bright, high-energy people into its ranks, neither can it afford to be indecisive, because it is full of action-oriented, maverick employees. These are the type of people who demand that decisions be made at higher levels or else they will take matters into their own hands. Therefore, the Coast Guard is forced to either have a well-thought-through decision-making process at the executive levels or be willing to encourage independent decision making at the customer-service levels. Interestingly enough, the Coast Guard does both.

At headquarters in Washington, D.C., and in larger districts around the nation, the admirals and senior officers employ the following classic, five-step decision-making process:

1. Gather information and understand the facts.
2. Involve all stakeholders in the process.
3. Consider various solutions and their consequences.
4. Ensure consistency with personnel policy and objectives.
5. Effectively communicate the decision.

Sometimes a small group is formed to work through the process. Sometimes a larger, more formal task force is created. Rarely, though, does an executive sitting in an ivory tower dictate an order that has a major impact on the entire Coast Guard (as decisions emanating from national headquarters tend to do). Rather, as many people as is reasonable are usually involved in formulating the final decision. That's because, in the Coast Guard, the filter between the policy-writer and the doer is as thin as a single sheet of paper. And if a stupid decision is issued, so much flak is received that the decision will be either ignored or rescinded. Rather than experience such an embarrassment, Coast

Guard executives are careful to adhere to the proper process and involve as many people as possible. Doing so cuts the risk of making a poor decision and increases the probability that a decision will be well received. And in theory, the more people involved in formulating a decision, the more supporters there will be once it has been communicated to the masses.

There are, of course, exceptions. Sometimes a problem crops up where the solution is so obvious, with so much natural built-in support that forming a task force or taking too much time to make the decision would be counter-productive. In such a case, the Commandant of the Coast Guard may issue what is called a "stroke of the pen" decision, where a quick white paper or brief memo is sent out announcing the decision and ordering the change. Even then, however, the decision-making process is adhered to. Performing those five steps may take a few hours or a few months depending upon the complexity of the issue. But if followed, the five steps almost always result in a positive outcome.

At the other extreme, there are times when decisions cannot possibly be made in an office and someone must be at the scene. For situations like this, teams are sent to the field to evaluate the situation and take appropriate action. Good examples are the Coast Guard's Strike Force teams, which typically deploy after major pollution incidents (oil spills, chemical releases, and so forth) and perform a variety of Environmental Protection Agency functions (such as air and water quality monitoring). There are four Strike Force teams nationwide: the Gulf Strike Force in Mobile, Alabama; the Pacific Strike Force in Novato, California; the Atlantic Strike Force in Fort Dix, New Jersey; and the National Strike Force in Elizabeth City, North Carolina. Each team is made up of thirty-nine members who are on twenty-four-hour, seven-day watch.

Most of the time, Coast Guard personnel in the field are not encumbered with having to call back to headquarters every time a decision needs to be made. Nor are there too many rules put in place, which might tend to hamstring people or box them in. Rather, Coasties are encouraged to anticipate events, use discretion, and make decisions based on their own best judgment. And that type of encouragement almost always produces good results.

In January 2001, for instance, a helicopter team in Alaska received word that a fishing vessel was taking on water and appeared to be in some trouble. When the Coasties arrived at the scene, however, the crew of the boat indicated that they really didn't need any help and waved the Coast Guard away. In the helicopter, the crew talked over the situation.

"They've got all their crab pots in the stern of the ship, which is causing them to ride low."

"Yeah, and they're looking at 40-foot seas, high winds, rain, and ice."

"I'd say they're going to be calling us again."

"Yeah, there's no way they're going to make it."

Rather than flying back to home base, an hour away, the pilot made arrangements to land at a remote island only ten minutes away. Less than an hour later, the fishing vessel made an emergency call:

"Coast Guard! Coast Guard! Mayday! Mayday! We've just taken a big wave and are going down! Come get us."

When the chopper got back on scene, the members of the boat crew had their wet suits on and were waiting to be pulled off the deck. Shortly after they were safely in the helicopter, the fishing vessel sank. And on the way back to base, one of the fishermen had a heart attack and received prompt first aid treatment from his rescuers.

Because the helicopter crew had the discretion to use their own best judgment, they were able to get back on scene in only ten minutes. Had they not made that crucial decision, the fishing vessel would have sunk, and all four members of the crew would surely have either drowned or died of hypothermia. Instead, they all survived.

The Coast Guard is an organization filled with leaders, and leaders, by their very nature, are action-oriented people. So the Coast Guard encourages decisive action not only because it is mission-driven by the core value of Devotion to Duty, but also because its personnel are naturally inclined to act on their own.

It's a good lesson for any executive: If you bring people into your organization who are expected to act, then you had better let them do so. What's more, if you encourage action, then you breed engagement and commitment, inspire participation and involvement, and keep job satisfaction high.

In encouraging its people to make decisions, the Coast Guard also holds them accountable for the decisions they make. Leaders are allowed to use discretion based on the situations they encounter. But when a mistake is made, or when normal procedures are violated during the course of an operation, even though the mission may have been completed successfully, a formal investigation will be held and tough questions will be asked: "Did your crew have the proper training? Were they compatible? Were they rested? Are you sure the conditions you encountered justified your decision? Would you do it differently if you had to do it over again? How could you have done things better? In the end, do you believe you did the right thing?"

That being said, every Coast Guard leader in the field knows that their commanding officer at headquarters has a standing order for them: "Do what you have to do. Act first. Call me later."

On the sea at night, away from the ambient lights of civilization, you can see breathtaking views of stars, constellations, and galaxies. And the moonrise can look just like a sunrise, only in blues and violets rather than yellows and reds. Lieutenant J. M. found he could sit up all night just to watch the sky. But at midnight on 14 July 2001, while on the bridge of the USCGC *Cushing*, his momentary glance upward was interrupted when a go-fast boat sped across the ship's bow.

"There it is!" he shouted. "Let's go!"

Having been alerted to a possible drug run, the 110-foot cutter was patrolling the waters just east of the British Virgin Islands. For the next twenty minutes, the *Cushing* pursued the go-fast boat as it tried all sorts of high-speed maneuvers to avoid the cutter's searchlights. Suddenly, though, the go-fast appeared to hit a 5-foot wave swell and then stopped dead in the water. What happened next stunned Lt. J. M. and his crew of sixteen.

It turned out that the boat was not loaded with drugs. It was loaded with immigrants. The high-speed chase had apparently frightened them so much that about twenty had come up from below deck. But this 28-foot pleasure boat was built to hold only seven or eight people comfortably. So when the immigrants pushed toward the stern, the boat capsized. Suddenly, the *Cushing* was surrounded by people screaming in the darkness and flailing about in the water. None of them had lifejackets and many, apparently, did not know how to swim.

The *Cushing* was now confronted with a search and rescue case rather than one of law enforcement. Crew members immediately threw life jackets, rings, life rafts, and just about anything else that would float into the water. Then they leaned over the railings and began pulling people on board. From the bridge, Lt. J. M. and his executive officer surveyed the situation from a broader view. As they shined the searchlight on the scene, the lieutenant spotted what appeared to be a baby floating face down in the water.

The lieutenant knew that somebody was going to have to go into the water to get that baby (a violation of standard procedure). But he couldn't just yell an order from the bridge, because the crew wouldn't know what to do. So he decided to leave the bridge and go down to the deck (also a violation of standard procedure).

"You've got the bridge," he told the XO. "Don't push the clutch in. Just stay right here. Keep the light on the baby."

"Aye, aye, sir."

Once on deck, the lieutenant pointed toward the child. Three members of the crew (Dennis and Ken, two petty officers; and Harry, a fireman) volunteered to go into the water. "Go!" shouted the skipper, even though he knew full well that, given the conditions, the men might not be able to make it back. What he did know, however, was that the baby would surely die if he didn't let them try.

Dennis reached the child in a matter of minutes and swiftly brought her back to the crew. After a few minutes of receiving CPR, the child took a breath. "She's alive, sir!" one of the workmen shouted to the skipper. "She's alive!" Meanwhile, Ken and Harry were helping immigrants into the life rafts and onto the cutter. Harry actually took off his lifejacket and put it on a woman who couldn't swim.

The entire episode happened so fast that no one had time to think. They only had time to act. When it was all over, twenty-two of the twenty-six immigrants aboard the boat had been saved by the heroism of the *Cushing*'s crew. Four people, however, lost their lives, including the mother and seven-year-old brother of the baby who was saved. Upon returning to port, Lt. J. M. wrote up his report. He put every detail into it, including his violations of procedure. And sure enough, a full investigation was conducted regarding his actions. Two months later, he was cleared of all charges.

"I didn't really sweat the investigation," said the lieutenant. "We work for a great organization. We did our job, and we'd do it again. Once we saw her, we weren't going to let that baby die. That's not who the Coast Guard is. I knew everything would be all right."

And it was. Later that year, Lt. J. M. received the Coast Guard

Foundation Award for Heroism. He shared it with his shipmates. The little girl first seen floating face down in the water spent three days recuperating in the hospital, where doctors said she had been within thirty seconds of death. A native of Colombia, she was ultimately granted entrance into the United States and went to live with her aunt in San Francisco. When she turns eighteen, her college education will be aided by a scholarship fund started by the crew of the USCGC *Cushing*.

The Coast Guard on Leadership

Encourage Decisiveness

- Action-oriented people demand that decisions be made at higher levels, or else they will take matters into their own hands.
- Have a well-thought-through decision-making process at the executive levels of your organization and encourage decision making at the customer-service levels.
- Follow this five-step decision-making process:
    1. Gather information and understand the facts.
    2. Involve all stakeholders in the process.
    3. Consider various solutions and their consequences.
    4. Ensure consistency with personal policy and objectives.
    5. Effectively communicate the decision.
- Make the filter between the policy-writer and the doer as thin as a single sheet of paper.
- Issue "stroke of the pen" decisions when it appears that forming a task force or taking too much time is unwarranted.
- Too many rules get in the way of leadership and decision making. They tend to hamstring or box in leaders.
- Encourage people to anticipate events, use discretion, and make decisions based on their own best judgment.
- If you bring people into your organization who are expected to act, then you must let them do so.
- Encouraging action breeds engagement and commitment, inspires participation and involvement, and keeps job satisfaction high.
- Hold people accountable for their decisions. Conduct investigations when warranted.
- Make it a standing order to "Act first. Call me later."

Chapter 11

Empower the Young

Take this patrol boat and a crew of fifteen people into the North Pacific
and perform all Coast Guard missions in accordance with policies
and procedures—and bring them all back safe and sound.

—Coast Guard commanding officer to a twenty-four-year-old
lieutenant, Bodega Bay, California

The first time I was out there and everything was on my shoulders, I felt
scared and nervous. Then, after I got some experience
under my belt, it became second nature.

—A twenty-six-year-old Coast Guard "veteran"

The Coast Guard's Marine Safety Offices have people on hand in every major
seaport in the United States, checking ship manifests, maintaining safety standards, and inspecting cargo. Many different federal regulations govern materials
allowed into the country, and the Coast Guard is responsible for enforcing

every one of them. So Coasties have to be educated on all those laws and trained to recognize the materials when they see them, and then have to feel skilled and confident enough to deal with people who violate the law.

In the summer of 2001, two Coast Guard inspectors (aged twenty-four and twenty-six) were conducting normal spot-check investigations at a cargo facility at one of the largest seaports on the eastern seaboard. As crates came off the ships, the inspectors would choose several at random and have them opened. One of those crates was filled with canisters of ammonium nitrate, a chemical used in fertilizer, which can be mixed with diesel fuel to make a blasting agent. This substance was used in the bombing of the Murrah Federal Building in Oklahoma City.

All Coast Guard port inspectors are encouraged to use discretion regarding whatever action they take upon finding illegal materials. They are, after all, dealing with big corporations and a multi-billion-dollar business. Sometimes it's appropriate to simply issue a citation and either isolate or confiscate the materials. But ammonium nitrate is a major threat. Unchecked, it has the potential to cause a major explosion at the port. So the two young inspectors immediately ordered a halt to operations at this particular cargo facility. All cargo had to be visually inspected for additional illegal materials. The ammonium nitrate had to be dealt with. And nothing was permitted to leave the cargo facility until those two action items were completed.

Needless to say, these orders caused consternation among the various executives who ran the cargo facility, the shipping company, and the receiving company. One top executive called the Coast Guard captain of the port and complained about "these two young people who are overreacting and costing us thousands of dollars."

The captain then spoke with the two young inspectors and heard what they had to say. "You've done the right thing," he told them. "I'll cover your backs. I'm also sending some more help your way. Take as much time as you need to secure the facility. Good job."

Upon completion of the operation, the Coast Guard determined that the shipping company had simply slacked off. They did not request or obtain the proper permits for transportation of such hazardous cargo. There was no deliberate attempt to harm, just people trying to save money and get out of a little work. Accordingly, the Coast Guard fined the shipping company $200,000.

How many professional organizations do you know that would put a twenty-four- or twenty-six-year-old in charge of hazardous materials inspection at a major seaport? How many would put a twenty-five-year-old in charge of a ship with a crew and a life-or-death mission, or helicopter crew on a search and rescue mission?

It happens all the time in the U.S. Coast Guard.

An operational commander in Woods Hole, Massachusetts, will tell a young officer: "Here's a 110-foot patrol boat. You're responsible for these thousand square miles of ocean and everything that happens in it. I don't know what your mission is going to be tomorrow, but take that ship the Coast Guard just gave you and go do the right thing." A CO in Bodega Bay, California, will tell a young lieutenant: "Take this patrol boat and a crew of fifteen people into the North Pacific and perform all Coast Guard missions in accordance with policies and procedures—and bring them all back safe and sound."

All around the nation, people in their twenties are performing jobs that really matter. A young enlisted woman in Port Angeles, Washington, is standing a twelve-hour watch alone at night, handling radio communications, monitoring emergency calls, deploying cutters, and launching helicopters when called for. A twenty-one-year-old enlisted man is being dropped out of a helicopter in 20- to 30-foot seas to help a sinking boat. A nineteen-year-old is holding a gun on a drug runner off the coast of Florida. Another is pulling immigrants who haven't eaten in days off flimsy rafts in the Mona Pass and administering first aid to them.

There's no doubt about it. The Coast Guard is a very young service. The average age of personnel below the rank of admiral is in the twenties. But the fact that the organization empowers young people and gives them the opportunity to act is partly due to necessity. People who jump out of helicopters in 20- to 30-foot seas have to be young. No one wants people in their fifties performing such a task. But remember also that the Coast Guard has a very small number of active personnel compared to the magnitude of its missions. And when there's a shortage of people, everybody has to step up to the plate. Not only are young people expected to perform, the organization demands that they do so. There are no spectators in the Coast Guard.

Empowering young people is also a smart, open-minded organizational strategy. It's a mark of youth to be idealistic, committed, and innovative, to think that "we can do this better." Young people are energetic, which allows more things to get done. They also tend to keep the organization imbued with vibrancy and vitality. If guided properly, a young person may achieve twice as much as someone in their fifties.

The downside, of course, is that young people are also inexperienced. Consequently, the tendency of most large organizations is to limit their impact. Executives usually start them out slow and give them menial jobs. They don't want to give a twenty-something anything very important because they don't want to risk mistakes being made.

The Coast Guard approaches the situation differently. It has put in place five key organizational elements that facilitate young people being successful once they are empowered:

1. Provide technical training needed to be successful. Crucial expertise and competence are imparted at Cape May, the Coast Guard Academy, and at Training Centers at Petaluma, California; Yorktown, Virginia; Mobile, Alabama; and Elizabeth City, North Carolina.
2. Provide mentoring. It is part of the job of chiefs and senior officers to advise, guide, and counsel younger personnel under their immediate supervision.
3. Allow mistakes. Action-oriented people will make mistakes. Intelligent people gain knowledge and grow from their mistakes. As one senior admiral advises: "Let people make some mistakes. That's how they learn."
4. Provide encouragement and support. Headquarters encourages its people to take action and backs them up when they do so. If the troops in the field know they are going to be supported by their command, they will gain the confidence and courage needed to perform their jobs well.
5. Bestow trust. People who are empowered must be trusted to do the job as they see fit. When people are trusted, they more fully respect

their leaders, their organizations, and their missions. Respect is a by-product of trust.

The Coast Guard gives young people authority and empowers them to act. And time and time again, they rise to the occasion and come through like champions. Recall that, when selecting team members, the Coast Guard searches for seven qualities in each individual: intelligence, high energy, self-confidence, continual learning, compassion, courage with a bias toward action, and character. These are the type of people who tend to thrive in an environment where they are allowed to try new things, where they're allowed to learn by failing once in a while, where they're empowered to take action, and where they're allowed to do what they think is best.

"The first time I was out there and everything was on my shoulders, I felt scared and nervous," recalled one twenty-six-year-old Coast Guard "veteran." "Then, after I got some experience under my belt, it became second nature. I'd rather be out here running this small boat station than in a big company making copies. I feel like I'm doing something good, like I'm making a difference. And I know I'm accomplishing stuff. That makes a big difference to me."

"The Coast Guard challenges me," said another. "They keep my mind going. I get to learn and have new experiences. And you know what? If I ever decide to move on, I'll have a whole lot more experience on my resume than the average twenty-five-year-old. Some of the things the Coast Guard lets me do are unbelievable. If the job ever gets boring, I'll find something else to do. But, for now, I'm still here."

One of the best things a leader can say to a young person is: "I trust you. Go do what you feel is the right thing to do."

Come to think of it, that is one of the best things a leader can say to a person of any age.

The Coast Guard received a call reporting that a couple of people were drowning off the Steel Pier in Atlantic City. Word was immediately relayed to a 21-foot boat patrolling about a half-mile away. "We're on our way," confirmed the coxswain, a twenty-one-year-old third-class boatswain's mate less than two years out of Cape May.

Upon arrival, he and his two-person crew (which included a second-class machinery technician and a seaman apprentice) spotted a ten-year-old boy flailing about in the surf. He had apparently been caught in a rip tide. Coast Guard policy, however, did not allow this type of boat into the surf zone because of the risk to the crew. "I think we should go in there," the coxswain said to his shipmates. "What do you think?"

"Let's go get that kid!" they responded.

So the coxswain steered his boat into the dangerous surf. But when they pulled the child out, they found his thirty-five-year-old mother underneath. Completely submerged, she was valiantly holding her son above the surface so he could breathe. The two crew members immediately pulled the woman out of the water and got her into the boat. The child, in an apparent state of shock, was suffering from hypothermia and in need of immediate medical care. The mother was unconscious, not breathing at all, and had only a faint pulse.

While the crew administered rescue breathing and CPR to the victims, the coxswain knew he had to act quickly. There was an EMS ambulance on the beach and it was obvious that would be the quickest way to get the woman and child the medical attention they needed. Once again, however, Coast Guard policy barred this particular boat from being driven onto the beach. But this was a matter of life and death.

"I'm going to go straight for that ambulance and beach the boat," he said to his team members attending the victims. "Okay?"

"Yeah! Go for it!" they replied. "She will never survive the twenty-minute ride to the dock."

The coxswain then timed the waves just right, rode the surf onto the beach and, in a matter of minutes, got the victims to the ambulance, where they were whisked away to the hospital. No damage was done to the boat and no member of the crew was harmed. Unfortunately, the mother later died, but the ten-year-old boy survived.

In the natural course of events, the station CO initiated an investigation and filed a mishap report. That report affirmed the correctness of the decision while noting that the occasions on which beaching is warranted occur very rarely. Afterward, care was taken to prevent this good decision from becoming a precedent for future bad decisions: training was conducted to ensure that the crew knew the importance of each factor in their decision.

The Coast Guard on Leadership

Empower the Young

- Allow young people to perform jobs that really matter.
- Expect young people to perform well, and demand it of them.
- Empowering young people is a smart, open-minded organizational strategy. Their energy allows more things to get done and keeps the organization imbued with vibrancy and vitality.
- Put in place these five organizational elements to facilitate young people being successful once they are empowered:
    1. Provide technical training
    2. Provide mentoring
    3. Allow mistakes
    4. Provide encouragement and support
    5. Bestow trust.
- Young people thrive in an environment where they are allowed to learn by failing once in a while, where they're empowered to take action, and where they're allowed to do what they think is best.
- One of the best things you can say to a young person is: "I trust you. Go do what you feel is the right thing to do."

Chapter 12

Give the Field Priority

Rather than anchoring vessels within the harbors, it will be necessary for
you to play along the coasts in the neighborhood of your station. . . .
To fix yourself constantly or even generally at one position
would, in a great measure, defeat the purpose of the
establishment. It would confine your
vigilance to a particular spot.

—Alexander Hamilton, 4 July 1791

When you're out there on a dark and stormy night, I don't want you to
think about what the operations boss or the commanding officer
would want you to do. I want you to think about what you're
going to do. Make your own decision. It's your crew,
your position, your decision.

—Coast Guard commanding officer, Air Station
Atlantic City, New Jersey

In July 2001, two small planes took off from the southern side of the Alaskan Peninsula just below Amber Bay. The pilot in the lead plane had made this flight hundreds of times before. He owned a fishing cabin on the northern side of the peninsula and was taking several couples out for a week of vacation. In his plane, two women sat in the back and one of his buddies was up front with him. It was only supposed to be an hour-long flight. But as the two planes headed up one of the mountain passes, clouds unexpectedly settled in to create a very low ceiling. The closer they got to the mountains, the lower the ceiling became. To make matters worse, the winds whipping through the pass were unusually strong. Both planes were getting bounced around pretty hard, and visibility was rapidly fading. The pilot in the second plane got on the radio. "This is too bad," he said. "I'm turning around."

"I can make it," replied the lead pilot. "Besides, I've gone too far to turn back now. I couldn't make a one-eighty if I wanted to, there's not enough turn radius."

The second pilot turned his plane around, headed back to the south, up the coast, and around the mountains. It was an extra fifty or sixty miles, but it was a safer flight. When he arrived at the cabin, there was no sign of the first plane. "Oh no," he thought, "he must have gone down." So the second pilot called the Coast Guard and took off again to search for his friends.

At Air Station Kodiak, the whoopee alarm sounded within moments of the distress call. It was around ten o'clock at night, but there was plenty of light at this time of year in Alaska. A C-130 search plane took off and headed for the general area. Flying back and forth over the location at 6,000 feet, however, proved fruitless because the cloud cover prevented any visual sighting. So the two H-60 helicopters dispatched to the site had to take over. The senior pilot, a lieutenant named Scott, took charge of the operation. "We'll go through the pass and see if we can find them," he radioed to the pilot of the other chopper. "You guys take the east side and we'll take the west."

As they began searching, the pilot of the C-130 radioed that they had picked up the ELT (Emergency Locating Transmitter) signal from the

downed plane. "It's a fairly strong signal," she said. "We've done triangula-
tion and pinpointed the exact location. He either landed on the side of a
mountain or he crashed there. You are not very far away. Here are the
coordinates, but based on the cloud cover, I think they're too high for you
to get to them."

Scott's copilot punched the coordinates into the computer. Then the
two pilots took their helicopters up the canyon very slowly. As they got
higher they were surrounded by snow-capped mountains. They searched
back and forth repeatedly, making tight hairpin turns while gusts of twenty-
five- to thirty-mile-per-hour winds swept down the slopes and pushed them
around.

At about one in the morning, they were getting low on fuel and the conditions were so dangerous that Scott had to call off the search for that
moment. They slowly made their way back out to King Salmon, where they
landed at about 2:30 A.M. Little did Scott know that they had come within
900 yards of the downed plane, close enough for any survivors to hear the
engine noise. . . .

When new recruits go through the early indoctrination program at
Cape May, their company commanders will, at some point, take
them all out to the beach and face them toward the water. "That is your
office," they will say. "Most of your time in the Coast Guard will not be
spent sitting behind a desk. You will be in the field, usually at sea. The field
is your office. The field is your domain."

This concept of having most Coast Guard personnel in the field came
from one of America's great early leaders. Alexander Hamilton had traveled with the colonial army during the American Revolution. He had been
at Trenton, at Valley Forge, and at Yorktown. He had seen his leader,
George Washington, riding to the sound of the guns, inspiring the troops
with his presence, and personally confirming that victory had been
achieved. Hamilton knew the importance of being in the field as opposed
to being holed up in an office at headquarters. So when he created the
Revenue-Marine in 1790, he put in place a system that ensured his organization would maintain a major presence close to the people it served.

"[Rather than] anchoring vessels within the harbors," wrote Hamilton to his officers, "it will be necessary for you to play along the coasts in the neighborhood of your station. . . . To fix yourself constantly or even generally at one position would, in a great measure, defeat the purpose of the establishment. It would confine your vigilance to a particular spot."

More than two centuries later, the modern Coast Guard lives by that advice. With over 200 field offices around the United States, more than 95 percent of active duty personnel are not "anchored" at corporate headquarters. Their offices are in the field in the "neighborhood" of their "stations." They do not confine their "vigilance" to "one particular spot." By strategically positioning themselves throughout the nation, Coast Guard personnel are able to perpetuate the original "purpose of their establishment," which is to serve the American public.

Some executives, cooped up at headquarters all day, tend to forget that being in the field where their clients and customers are, where the organization's troops perform their work, is a fundamental tenet of leadership. George Washington was in the field with the troops all six years of the American Revolution. During the Civil War, Abraham Lincoln became the only sitting president to come under actual enemy fire. And Martin Luther King, Jr. was marching with the people during the civil rights movement, at Montgomery, at Birmingham, at Selma, and at Memphis.

People naturally think of their leaders as being out there in front, leading the charge, setting the example. The best leaders make traveling with the troops a habit. They know that it facilitates three things that keep their organizations stronger and more efficient:

1. Relationships and alliances. The simple act of spending time with people increases personal human contact, which, in turn, leads to trust and respect.
2. Decision making. Leaders are able to obtain vital facts and information necessary to make informed, accurate, and timely decisions.
3. Action. Setting the example inspires people to take action on their own initiative.

With such an emphasis on being close to the people they serve, it's not surprising that another key element of the Coast Guard's leadership philosophy is to give the field preference in just about everything. The field especially is given a strong role in setting policy and making on-site decisions.

Many large organizations make the fatal mistake of having planners at headquarters set policy for everybody else. However, when people in the field are not consulted in the policy-making process, they become enormously frustrated and resentful. That's because no one likes to be told what to do. And nearly everyone's first reaction to change, if they haven't been previously engaged, is negative.

The Coast Guard attempts to avoid such negative reactions (and create workable policies) by involving field commanders in just about all policy-making decisions. Not only does this make a huge difference in keeping the Coast Guard from doing ill-informed things at national headquarters, it also eliminates the old aphorism, "I'm from headquarters and I'm here to help you." In reality, things operate the other way around. Field commanders are brought to headquarters to help headquarters formulate policy.

However, maintaining such a guiding principle takes an ongoing, dynamic effort, largely because executives at headquarters have a natural tendency to forget what it's like to be in the field. The principle can only be maintained if the top executive holds fast and insists that field personnel be given priority in the policy-making process.

"When I have to sign off on a major policy decision," says the Commandant of the Coast Guard, "the first thing I ask is, 'What do the field commanders have to say about this?' No one would dare give me something without their input because they know I'd just toss it back at them. The bottom line is that I don't want our people in the field to feel that headquarters is something superior to them. They're the ones who are doing the job and putting their lives on the line. I want them to know I respect them and will follow their lead."

In terms of taking appropriate actions while on missions, almost no one tells field personnel how to handle their jobs. Coasties work as a team to make decisions and to do what is necessary in virtually every aspect of their day-to-day business.

At small boat stations, for instance, the people on site are responsible for the administration relating to all personnel, all equipment, and all missions. The boat crews, themselves, usually consist of anywhere from three to seven members, depending on the size of the boat. They work an average of eighty-four to ninety-six hours a week and are on duty twenty-four hours a day, seven days a week. When they take leave depends on how many qualified people are on location.

Every individual who goes out on a boat must be both properly trained and formally certified. Boarding teams, for example, are required to be law enforcement–qualified. Others must be schooled in hazardous materials clean-up, safety regulations, and CPR, among other things. In addition, boat crews must be under way within thirty minutes of a call. But most make it out in less than five to ten minutes because everybody helps each other get ready, just as they were trained to do in boot camp. The only difference is, at Cape May, the two-minute turnaround drill was just that, a drill. At a small boat station, it's real. It can and often does mean the difference in saving someone's life. When the crew is on the water, the team concept takes over and everybody has an input into decisions. One person, the coxswain, makes the final call if there's not a consensus.

Aircraft flight crews are also given priority in the decision-making process when they are on site. Because they never really know what to expect, and because unexpected situations often arise, it is just not feasible to be calling back to headquarters all the time. Rather, any member of the team may (and should) speak up at any time. Like the small boat crews, the rest of the helicopter team will stop and talk about it and then try to make a collective decision. Often a pilot in the air will do what the rescue swimmer in the water wants him to do. In such a case, it is the rescue swimmer who is closer to the field situation, therefore, the rescue swimmer must be given priority. Furthermore, nearly all commanding officers of Coast Guard air stations make it abundantly clear that they do not want the aircraft commanders to be calling back to headquarters for every little thing.

"When you're out there on a dark and stormy night," one captain tells all the pilots in his unit, "I don't want you to think about what the operations boss or the commanding officer would want you to do. I want you to think about what you're going to do. Make your decision. It's your crew, your position, your decision."

The ability to trust people under your authority is one of the best qualities of leadership. When you give the field priority, you not only get the job done better, but you, as a leader, gain more credibility for yourself. As a result, the entire organization flourishes.

—————

... Back in Alaska, a first-class petty officer and rescue swimmer named Bob was on twenty-four-hour call for any emergencies that might arise. He was asleep at his house in Kodiak when the phone rang at three in the morning.

"We've got a plane down near Amber Bay," said the officer of the day. "Got to relieve a crew that worked most of the night. Probably be leaving at 0400. Tim said he'd take it because your shift is almost over."

"No, it's my call, I'll go," responded Bob, who then leaped out of bed.

"Where are you going?" asked his wife.

"SAR case."

Twenty minutes later, Bob was at the base gathering his gear and huddling with his fellow crew members. There was Russ, a commander and the pilot in charge of the aircraft. Andy was a lieutenant and copilot. The flight mechanic was John, a petty officer third-class. As the four discussed their game plan and went through the preflight check, they all had very serious looks on their faces. Each knew they were heading into a dangerous area. Each knew their lives depended on one another, as did the lives of the people in the downed plane if, indeed, they were still alive.

After the helicopter took off, Bob lay down in the back to "get his mind right." He thought about all the procedures, what difficulties they might encounter, what would have to be done, the weather report. When they landed at King Salmon, Scott and his crew were there to provide a detailed briefing. "Here's where they are on the map. Here's what you're going to encounter. Be careful of the winds in this area. They're really rough. The cloud cover was really low. You've got to go unbelievably slow. When you get to this point on the map, you might be able to pick up their signal."

The rescue helicopter took off at six. The sun had come up and they had full daylight. They flew along Bristol Bay then up Pumice Creek. Slowly. Arduously. Russ, the aircraft commander, was in the front left seat; Andy, the other officer, in the right front. Bob and John, the crewmen, were in the back with the sliding door wide open. Everybody watched the ground closely.

"I've got a signal," yelled Andy. "Up ahead to the right. We must be close." But as soon as they moved up in elevation, snow began to fall. So they went back down the canyon about 800 feet, landed on a flat spot, and shut down the helicopter engine. "Let's hold for a little while," said Russ. "Maybe the snow will move out."

"Can't wait too long," commented Andy. "If there's anybody up there still alive, they're going to need rescuing."

"Tell you what," said Russ, "when we start back up, you focus on the right side of the cliff and I'll reference something down in the valley. That way, if we hit a white-out condition, you'll be able to take control of the chopper and get us out of here."

"Roger that," replied Andy.

Thirty minutes later, an opening in the clouds appeared and they took off again. Slowly they climbed through the clouds and back up the canyon. At an elevation of about 3,700 feet, they spotted the wreckage of the small plane. "There it is!" said Andy. "Let's fly over slow and have a good look."

The plane was perched precariously on the side of the mountain. It was a very steep grade on a treacherous terrain of heavy shale. The plane had rolled on its side upon impact, the entire front section had been crushed, and the wing was folded back. "Bob, what do you think?" asked Andy.

"I'd be hard-pressed to think anybody lived through that," he responded. "That's pretty brutal."

"Well, what do you want to do, Bob?" said Russ. "Do you want to go down?"

"Well, yeah. I'd like to go check it out just in case anybody's alive."

"All right, then."

Bob grabbed the helicopter's crash axe. "This has a sharp point on the end and I'll need it to dig into the shale so I can get up the side of that mountain," he said to John as the flight mechanic rigged him into the harness.

"How's this spot?" asked Russ after taking the helicopter down the mountain about 300 feet.

"Looks good," said Bob. "Once you guys let me down, I'm going to hang onto the mountain. Once you see me hanging on, you back off."

"Roger that."

John lowered Bob down with the hoist. He disconnected, and the chopper backed off and flew down another 500 feet and set down on a flat spot. The weather was nasty with misty snow and rain. The wind was blowing hard, and it was very cold. Bob started crawling up through the shale toward the plane. For every ten steps, he fell back seven. But he kept at it. And as he slowly crept up on the wreckage, he prepared himself mentally. "Oh, Lord," he prayed. "Get my heart ready for what I'm going to see. I've seen a lot of things, but I know this is going to be particularly bad. I pray you can get my heart right for this so I can do my job and function properly."

When Bob reached the front of the plane, he could see that the two guys up front had been killed instantly. The aircraft was a twisted, bloody mess. When he got around to the other side of the plane, he saw a hand come out of the window. It was the hand of a woman. She had been pushed back into the cargo department and folded so that her face was touching her legs. Her legs had been snapped and broken. She had survived fourteen hours in the wreckage, had lost a lot of blood, and was hypothermic.

"Hang on, ma'am," Bob said to her. "I'm going to get you out of there."

Then he got on the radiophone to his crew. "Game on, gentlemen. We've got a survivor."

"You're kidding!" Andy responded. "How many?"

"One, for now."

Bob didn't want to crawl inside because the plane was perched so precariously on the side of the mountain that he felt it might slide down with his weight added. Then he realized that the crash axe he had taken off the helicopter might cut through the fuselage. So he took his sleeping bag and used it to cushion the woman to make certain he didn't hit her. "This might hurt, ma'am, but I've got to squeeze this between your back and the plane so I don't hit you with the axe." Then, as he was packing the sleeping bag in, Bob noticed another woman underneath the first woman. She was unconscious and badly injured, but she was breathing.

That just spurred Bob on. The axe cut through the plane better than expected. "Thank God for this crash axe," he thought. But the vibrations caused both women to start groaning in pain. He couldn't hit too hard because he was afraid he might knock the plane off the side of the mountain. Within a half-hour, he had cut a section from the side of the plane all the way down to the bottom that was wide enough to get the women out. While cutting, he had to bang through the brake cable and get the landing gear out of the way. "There's a piece of landing gear coming your way," he radioed to the helicopter 1,000 feet below.

"Okay, let it go," came the response.

Bob dropped the landing gear down the side of the mountain and then peeled back the plane's fuselage like a tin can until he could get the first woman out. Having a tough time getting his footing in the shale, Bob finally pulled her out, laid her down above the wreckage, and covered her with a blanket. He noticed that the entire orbital around her left eye was smashed. She was conscious, so Bob began speaking to her to keep her mind off the pain. He identified himself and asked her what her name was.

"Linda," came the whispered response.

"Okay, Linda. I'm going to have to check on your friend. What is her name?"

"Ellen," she said.

When Bob got a good look at Ellen, he knew she was in serious trouble. Unconscious, she had a terrible pelvic injury, and Bob knew that such injuries resulted in death 60 to 70 percent of the time. Better to leave her where she was for the moment than try to move her without help.

"I have another woman alive up here," he radioed.

"We've sent for a mountain rescue team out of Juneau," said Andy.

"Cancel it," Bob responded. "These two women don't have four hours. We need people right now."

"Roger. We'll get on it."

A few minutes later, Bob was administering first aid to Linda when he heard on the radio that Alaska state troopers had just been flown in and were down at the entrance to Pumice Creek. "We're going to need as much help as possible to get these women down fast," Bob radioed. "I'd like to have those state troopers."

"Okay, Bob," responded Russ. "I can go get them if that's your decision."

"That's what I would like, if you can go get them for me," Bob confirmed.

Bob did not know it at the time, but Andy, the copilot, and John, the flight engineer, were already headed up the mountain to help. Russ was in the helicopter all by himself and seated on the left side. But everything is set up for a single pilot to fly the chopper from the right side and not the left. In fact, it's a major breach of procedure for a pilot to operate an aircraft from the left side only. The engines were turning, the rotors running. Russ couldn't just jump over the console, there was no other pilot available, and the lives of two women were on the line. Time was of the essence. So Russ flew the helicopter down to pick up the state troopers.

Bob heard the helicopter take off and looked down the mountain just in time to see the copilot and flight engineer climbing the mountain toward him. "My God," he thought. "Russ might just have ended his career. He opted to save these women's lives and put his career in jeopardy to do it. Wow, what an awesome thing to do."

Inspired by the boldness of his aircraft commander, Bob resolved to dig even deeper within himself. He headed down the mountain to help Andy and John reach the wreckage with the stretcher they were carrying. Once back up top, they strapped Linda in, and the three of them slid on their rears down the side of the mountain, a thousand feet along shale and snow, until they got to the aircraft. Meanwhile, Russ had returned with the state troopers and was waiting there for them. The troopers were headed up the mountain as they were coming down.

Russ, Andy, and John loaded Linda into the helicopter and immediately flew her out to the closest hospital. Bob started his climb back up the mountain just as a new Coast Guard helicopter was flying in to transport Ellen. The rescue swimmer from that crew, Jason (a petty officer second-class), quickly followed Bob.

Once they all got up to the plane, Bob, Jason, and the state troopers had a brief discussion about how they were going to get Ellen out of the wreckage. Together they lifted her out and quickly strapped her into the litter. She had lost a lot of blood and everybody knew time was of the essence. One of the troopers suggested hoisting her out right there at the site.

"No, we can't," countered Bob. "It's just too dangerous. It could take the helicopter out and us along with it. I see what you see and I don't like it. But I'm not going to risk killing four or more people to save one. I'm sorry."

That decision was heart-wrenching for Bob, one he would never forget. But it was the right call. They got down the mountain as fast as they could and put Ellen in the helicopter, which flew her to the hospital. Then Bob,

Jason, and the troopers started back up the mountain one final time to recover the bodies of the two men in the front of the plane. On their way up, the snow stopped and the sun came out.

Ellen died en route to the hospital. Linda's husband, who was a passenger in the plane that turned around, met her at the hospital. She survived and eventually made a full recovery. Shortly thereafter, Linda's son wrote a letter to Air Station Kodiak. It read in part: "We're very grateful and thankful to you, the men and women of the Coast Guard at Kodiak, because of what you've done. You saved our mom." The letter remained posted for weeks.

When Russ returned to base, he reported his breach of protocol and received the full backing of his commanding officer. Russ was awarded the Distinguished Flying Cross.

Bob got back to Kodiak about nine that night. He had neither eaten nor had anything to drink all day long. His boots were full of water, from sweat alone. He almost had to peel his dry suit off and, in the end, had to throw it away. When he got home, his wife was waiting for him with a hug.

"How'd it go?" she asked.

"Rough," he replied. "Can't talk about it right now."

Bob was also awarded the Distinguished Flying Cross for heroism.

The crash axe was put back. It's still part of the helicopter.

The Coast Guard on Leadership

Give the Field Priority

- Make sure people in the organization do not spend most of their time behind a desk.
- Instead of anchoring yourself at headquarters, get out in the field and visit the troops.
- Put people in the field in the "neighborhood" of their "stations."
- Don't confine your vigilance to a particular spot.
- Traveling with the troops facilitates three things that keep your organization strong and efficient:
    1. Relationships and alliances
    2. Decision making
    3. Action.
- Consult field personnel before new policies that will affect them are planned and implemented.
- Make sure that people in the field do not feel headquarters is superior to them. Let them know you respect them and will follow their lead.
- Make people on site responsible for administration relating to personnel, equipment, and missions.
- Encourage teamwork when making decisions in the field.

PART FOUR

Ensure the Future

Chapter 13

Leverage Resources

We realize that because we're small, we can't do everything by ourselves. We therefore have a natural predisposition to leverage our resources by working with other agencies.

—Coast Guard commanding officer,
San Juan, Puerto Rico

There is a cooperative ethos deeply ingrained in the service. That ethos, and its resultant web of relationships, ensure that *someone* does the job effectively, efficiently, and promptly.

In the summer of 1999, the Coast Guard received intelligence from the Federal Bureau of Investigation that a boat carrying large amounts of illegal drugs was seven miles off the southern coast of Puerto Rico and heading north. The section commander responded immediately: "Well, we know where the boat is, and there's no point in waiting around. Let's go get them." So the Coast Guard intercepted and impounded the boat, confiscated a large amount of cocaine, and arrested four drug smugglers.

The next day, however, other law enforcement agencies complained that the Coast Guard was a one-man show. The other agencies were focused on gaining credit for the bust themselves, and they griped that the Coast Guard had gone out and done it without consulting them.

The Coast Guard's commanding officer in San Juan took the criticism in stride. He realized that all federal agencies are obliged to recognize the process for avoiding duplicate claims on drug seizures. Every time a drug bust is made, only one agency can get primary credit for that particular bust. Other agencies involved get an assist.

So the captain offered a new approach. From then on, the Coast Guard would give up the primary claim and accept the assist. His long-term hope was that he would create a win-win situation in which all the agencies would be better able to work together. In addition, he reasoned that the "team" would be able to get a lot more done in the war on drugs if it leveraged its resources by working more frequently and more efficiently with other agencies.

When informed of the captain's actions, the district commanding admiral concurred. "The Coast Guard does not need credit," he said. "We need interagency cooperation. That, in turn, will help us get the job done and achieve our mission. The captain made a good decision."

A few days before Thanksgiving 2000, a go-fast boat left the northern coast of South America (from Colombia) just after dark. Three men were transporting more than 660 kilos of cocaine to Puerto Rico. Their plan was to go as fast as possible overnight, rest quietly during the daylight hours, and then pick up the pace the next night. The route to Puerto Rico took them up through southeastern Caribbean waters shared by a variety of government entities, including the old British islands of Barbados, Grenada, and St. Vincent, and the British and U.S. Virgin Islands. That's why, when the Coast Guard first received intelligence from the FBI about this particular drug run, the Coasties immediately contacted law enforcement agencies in these countries and territories, which had organized themselves into a coalition known as the RSS (Regional Security System) nations.

The RSS nations immediately deployed the large C-26 reconnaissance airplane that had been given to them by the United States for counter-drug work. Flying at an altitude of 20,000 feet, the crew of the C-26 first detected the go-fast boat in the early afternoon about a hundred miles off the coast of Puerto Rico. It was stopped in the water and had a blue tarp covering the boat as a form of camouflage to avoid detection. All that afternoon and the next night (after the drug smugglers started moving again), the position of the boat was monitored alternately by the RSS C-26 and reconnaissance airplanes of the Coast Guard and Customs Service.

Coordinating the entire operation, the Coast Guard asked the British Drug Squad if they wanted to join the Customs Service to intercept the go-fast boat. They agreed to do so, while the Coast Guard provided a helicopter for support and the USCGC *Cushing* for backup. The *Cushing*'s job was to catch the drug smugglers if they decided to turn around and make a run for it back to South America.

The smugglers had planned to land on a remote southern shore of Puerto Rico in the early morning hours of Thanksgiving Day, hoping to catch all the law enforcement agencies napping on the holiday. But a few miles offshore, with the British Drug Squad and Customs interceptors and the Coast Guard helicopter closing in, the smugglers began tossing their drug bales overboard. By the time they were caught, they had no drugs left on board. Meanwhile, the Coast Guard had enlisted the aid of FURA (Forces United for Rapid Action), a local group consisting of the Puerto Rican Special Police and several tactical unit SWAT teams, to locate and arrest the drug smugglers' accomplices who were waiting on the beach with pick-up trucks to transport the cocaine inland.

In the end, the British Drug Squad and Customs received primary credit for the bust, while everybody else picked up an assist. Meanwhile, the *Cushing* had followed along and picked up all the drug bales, which were then used as evidence to convict the criminals in a trial held under Puerto Rican jurisdiction.

In the Caribbean and the Gulf of Mexico, it is routine for the Coast Guard to coordinate this sort of federal and international involvement. Almost all the drug interdiction cases are inclusive and cooperative. From experience, the Coast Guard has learned that it is really the best way to make meaningful progress on illegal drug traffic in the region. Such relationships have been formalized in more than twenty-five bilateral treaties between the United States and participating countries in the Caribbean, which allow cutters and aircraft to proceed at will directly into their territorial seas or fly into their sovereign airspace.

"We realize that, because we're small, we can't do everything by ourselves," said the commanding officer in San Juan. "We therefore have a natural predisposition to leverage our resources by working with other agencies."

Moreover, when the Coast Guard leverages all the international agencies in the Caribbean to work together by building teams and coalitions across all sorts of natural barriers, it helps strengthen the community of the entire region. This philosophy extends across the Coast Guard. Whether a sister military service, a fellow federal agency, a local port authority, or a partnership with a private association, the Coast Guard finds enormous value in promoting collaboration and goodwill. Just as good relationships within a small team make a difference, good relationships with other organizations result in greater chances for mission success.

By leveraging resources in this manner, the Coast Guard provides appropriate stewardship of American taxpayer dollars by making sure it gets the most bang for the buck. According to Coast Guard financial analyses, the organization routinely documents a six-to-one return on investment of taxpayer monies in terms of property and lives saved, drugs seized, and numbers of illegal immigrants that do not become a burden on the social system of the country.

The Coast Guard strategically pulls disparate agencies together to achieve a common goal. This line of thinking emanates from a cooperative ethos deeply ingrained in the service. That ethos, and its resultant web of relationships, assures that someone does the job effectively, efficiently, and promptly.

Coast Guard people have enough confidence and strength of character to put their egos on the back burner. They are willing and able to step back and work, both collectively and individually, as part of a team. They work with people rather than tell them what to do. They apply diversity, build alliances, and leverage resources in order to make something bigger happen, to achieve more, and to obtain a better overall result for the nation.

After Hurricane Lennie rocked Puerto Rico in early 2000, the port of San Juan was closed by the Coast Guard captain of the port (COTP) for a few days to clear the channel of debris and get things back in order. But right after reopening, a 605-foot Russian cargo freighter laden with cement, the *Sergo Sergozakariabze,* ran aground only twenty-five yards offshore of El Morro Castle, Puerto Rico's five-hundred-year-old fort and a world heritage site. In this environmentally sensitive area, the situation was compounded by a number of underwater archeological treasures near the grounded vessel and a shark breeding ground in the immediate vicinity.

The Coast Guard was responsible for removing the fuel from the vessel, a task that was accomplished in only four days. At that point, the organization had a decision to make: Walk away now, wait for the cement and other cargo to be removed, then return to supervise the removal of the vessel, or stay and coordinate the rest of the operation.

The Coast Guard decided to stay.

With environmental groups screaming, local politicians breathing down their necks, and the media constantly monitoring the situation, the Coast Guard led a process that brought more than thirty stakeholders together. They called in the Puerto Rican Department of Environmental Quality (responsible for oil spills), the Puerto Rican Department of Natural Resources (responsible for fish), the Puerto Rican Department of Tourism, the U.S. Fish and Wildlife Service, and numerous private corporations. Collectively, they developed a plan, and everybody worked together to implement it. Over the next four months, blasting had to be done to remove solid cement rubble. Air had to be monitored to prevent cement dust from affecting local communities. Water quality had to be monitored to make certain the shark breeding ground would not be harmed. And scientists had to make certain there would be no chemical reactions that might damage El Morro. After the removal of more than ten thousand tons of rubble, the *Sergo Sergozakariabze* floated up and was pulled away from the shore by tugboats.

The Coast Guard employed its expertise in teamwork and leveraging of resources to make everything work smoothly. On a daily basis, it made sure that every team member understood their role, had an active voice in what went on, and performed efficiently and with excellence. At the end of the day, everybody could claim credit for a successful operation.

The Coast Guard on Leadership

Leverage Resources

- The best way to make meaningful progress is to be inclusive and cooperative.
- You must realize that, if your organization is small, you can't do everything yourself.
- Develop a natural predisposition to leverage your resources by working with other organizations.
- When you build teams and coalitions across all sorts of natural barriers you strengthen the community of the entire region.
- By leveraging resources properly, you help make certain your organization gets the most bang for the buck.
- Concentrate on pulling disparate agencies together to achieve a common goal.
- A cooperative ethos in your organization assures that *someone* does the job effectively, efficiently, and promptly.
- Have enough confidence and strength of character to put your ego on the back burner.
- Be willing to step back and work, both collectively and individually, as part of a team.
- Work *with* people rather than tell them what to do.

Chapter 14

Sponsor Continual Learning

It will be particularly acceptable if the officers
improve the opportunities they have. . . .

—Alexander Hamilton, 4 July 1791

Honor comes in when you make a mistake and own up to it. Even if it
wasn't your fault, as the leader, you must take the responsibility.
When an incident happens, the best leaders will say: "Okay, we
had a problem. I'm not going to try to cover it up. Let's
look at it and find out if I made a mistake or was
negligent. If that's the case, I'll own up to it."

—Coast Guard commanding officer, small
boat station, Yorktown, Virginia

Fishing is a multi-billion-dollar industry that has a huge impact on the economy of the United States. The Coast Guard is responsible for enforcement of federal fishing laws in all U.S. waters, including the Atlantic and Pacific Oceans, the Gulf of Mexico, and the Bering Sea.

Coast Guard cutters patrol the waters and conduct random boardings of fishing vessels to make certain that laws are being obeyed, that fishermen are in the appropriate areas, that they have proper permits, that they are catching only the fish they are permitted to catch, and that they are under their allotted quotas. But it's not as easy a job as it might seem. When it comes to distinguishing types of fish, for instance, Coast Guard personnel must be able to tell the difference between flounder, halibut, sole, three different types of rockfish, five different types of salmon, and countless other species and their varieties. Also, a fish that brings forty to fifty cents a pound might look almost exactly like one that brings only two cents a pound.

In the early 1990s, fishermen began to complain that many Coast Guard personnel were making errors in their identification of fish and that some were not sufficiently familiar with the myriad complex fishing laws and regulations. So the Coast Guard conducted a fisheries enforcement study to get at the root of the problem. The report concluded in part that better, more formalized training and education needed to be put in place for Coast Guard boarding teams. So five "Fish Schools" were created and located strategically throughout the nation: Cape Cod, Massachusetts; Charleston, South Carolina; New Orleans, Louisiana; Kodiak, Alaska; and a West Coast school that travels between Washington, Oregon, California, and Hawaii.

Boarding teams from all over the Coast Guard attend these schools for three days at a time to learn everything about their jobs, including the identification of fish and types of fishing; laws and records; specific fishing areas; how to conduct boardings; how to write up various reports, fines, and citations; how to inspect log books; how to behave cordially and professionally; and so on. Each Fish School is run by the Coast Guard, and all instructors are active duty personnel who have served on fishing patrol boats with actual boarding experience. Most of the schools have about ten instructors on staff who rotate out every three to four years, as they would for any other assignment in the Coast Guard. They come in and go through their own educational process where they learn the subject matter, teach it to boarding crews, and then perpetuate the efficiency of the school by coaching the junior instructors on how to become experts.

Each instructor team in every Coast Guard Fish School, then, has a never-ending cycle of perpetual, continual learning built in. And that concept is applied to their students as well, because attending Fish School is not a one-time thing for active duty personnel. Because laws and regulations are constantly changing, boarding crews are required to take refresher training courses on a continuing basis. It's part of the Coast Guard philosophy of constant reminders, constant reinforcement, and continual learning.

L eadership and learning go hand in hand. All great leaders are continual learners. They learn from mistakes and experiences, conduct formal post-mortems, engage in ongoing intellectual study, and are unusually self-critical and self-analytical. Why do they do these things? Because leaders are constantly driving forward to achieve their goals, their visions, and their missions. And part of the drive forward is getting knocked back a time or two, failing once in a while. If they are to achieve things, then they must overcome defeat, learn from it, and move on.

The best leaders also create organizations where people are continually learning how to do their jobs better, where they are adapting to the changing times and creating new avenues to success. In contrast, organizations that do not have their people immersed in continual leaning programs tend to make the same mistakes over and over again. The fact is that an organization imbued with continual learning helps eliminate mistakes and increase results. Therefore, continual learning is a tool for achievement.

Continual learning also meets the basic human need to improve and grow. The very best organizations, public or private, large or small, provide numerous, ongoing opportunities for people to improve their skills and talents.

In the United States Coast Guard, the emphasis on learning is paramount. "A key goal in meeting the challenges ahead," says one senior officer, "is to establish a leadership and work environment that enables all people to reach their maximum potential." Accordingly, everywhere you turn in the Coast Guard, people are in the midst of acquiring new skills, gaining new knowledge, attending technical classes, and working toward advanced college degrees. When recruiting members to its team, the Coast Guard searches for people who are adaptable, flexible, and able to adjust to change quickly. The organization invariably selects bright people who are lifelong learners and then puts them in an environment where they can do just that, continually learn and grow.

At the Coast Guard Academy, as cadets learn the basic tenets of leadership, they are taught *how* to think, not what to think. And they are schooled in how to work with followers. "Your job is to ensure that your subordinates excel," they are told, "and that they have whatever money, materials, time, training, and direction are needed to do their jobs. Your job is to help them achieve their goals by giving them opportunities to learn and grow."

After cadets leave the Academy, and after new recruits complete their early indoctrination programs at Cape May, many go on to obtain further, specialized education at one of the Coast Guard's two major training facilities, in Yorktown, Virginia, and Petaluma, California. Together with other training facilities, these two units provide the skills and knowledge recruits need to perform the missions of the Coast Guard, including defense operations, search and rescue, aids to navigation, marine safety, maritime law enforcement, and marine environmental protection. People receive operational training in such things as boat operations, oil spill cleanup, emergency medical services (EMS), boarding of other vessels for inspection and/or seizure, and rescues at sea and on land. The Coast Guard also provides a full spectrum of training for support and service personnel, including food service, telephone and communications, electricians, and computer services.

While the Training Centers at Yorktown and Petaluma provide basic skills preparation early in the careers of Coasties, they also afford opportunities for classes over the course of a career that allow individuals to progress from apprentice to journeyman to master in their fields of expertise. And because of the rotation of jobs in the Coast Guard, the Training Centers are always filled to capacity because there are always people moving into new jobs that require expertise and specialized training. In any given year, more than half of active duty personnel take some sort of training at either Yorktown or Petaluma through classes at the facilities, traveling training courses on the road, or correspondence classes.

Other areas of ongoing training in the Coast Guard include the Leadership Development Center, which includes the Chief Petty Officer's

Academy at Petaluma and Officer Candidate School at the Coast Guard
Academy in New London. The Leadership Development Center provides
ongoing leadership training for all personnel in the Coast Guard through
special courses, programs, and traveling seminars presented at field units.
In addition, the Coast Guard encourages members to sign up for distance
learning programs on land and at sea through the use of modern technology and the Internet. The Coast Guard is so serious about this that it offers
to pay the cost of the education. Aviation specialists undergo entry-level
and advanced training at the Aviation Training Center in Mobile, Alabama,
and at the Aviation Technical Training Center in Elizabeth City, North
Carolina.

In major organizations, rapid changes in modern technology drive training and continual learning. To serve customers well, it is necessary to stay
up with society's latest changes and innovations. To adjust, many large corporations will hire new people with specialized expertise. In the Coast
Guard's case, however, rather than increasing the number of people in its
ranks, the organization, through training and education, chooses to first
transform those who are already there.

The size of the Coast Guard, in terms of people, is similar to what it was
thirty years ago, but the missions have changed with the times. In the
1970s, for instance, people called in distress pleas on radios. Now, most
use wireless telephones. So the Coast Guard made the switch to wireless
telephones. The organization also switched most lighthouses and buoys
to solar power and has experimented with low-maintenance fuel cell bat-
teries.

Many decades ago most cutters were designed for fisheries enforcement.
Now, in some cases, they must hold three hundred illegal immigrants. And
smaller boats have to be speedy enough to catch illegal drug runners on go-
fast boats. The Coast Guard adapted to each mission change. But new cutters and small boats require new skills in operations and maintenance.
Modern navigations systems, such as Global Positioning Systems (GPS) and
Dynamic Positioning Systems (DPS), are quite different from the old
method of plotting courses on charts by hand, so the Coast Guard trains
people in how to use them. State-of-the-art electronics dramatically change
maintenance and repair methods. Where wires used to be soldered, computer boards are now pulled out, worked on, and replaced.

As times change and sophisticated new equipment is put in place, people must be ready and able to use it. If they're not, the missions of the organization cannot be achieved. For the Coast Guard, that means that laws may be broken, homeland security will be at risk, and lives may be lost. Those are unacceptable results. Coast Guard leaders understand the importance of adaptability to new mission challenges, and have built that flexibility into the organization as a mandatory standard.

Coast Guard people are always trying to refine their processes. They are constantly thinking about how to make things work better. Due to the nature of the Coast Guard missions, and the fact that each person plays multiple roles in the process, continual education and training is a necessity if the organization is to survive and flourish.

But for all the formal training and specialized classes offered, the Coast Guard relies very heavily on "learning by doing." It's one thing to learn to drive a 44-foot boat in calm training conditions, and another thing altogether to operate it on a dark and stormy night when the lives of your crew are at stake. The Coast Guard believes that the field is the greatest classroom and on-the-job experience the greatest teacher. That's why the organization documents all missions with written reports and, in cases where lives were lost or procedures violated, performs in-depth post-mortem investigations.

"Honor comes in when you make a mistake and own up to it," says the CO of a small boat station to local boat commanders. "Even if it wasn't your fault, as the leader, you must take the responsibility. When an incident happens, the best leaders will say, 'Okay, we had a problem. I'm not going to try to cover it up. Let's look at it and find out if I made a mistake or was negligent. If that's the case, I'll own up to it.'"

The Coast Guard's willingness to investigate itself, even when it hurts, and then to broadcast the lessons learned, is a very intelligent thing for an organization to do. It decreases the probability of future mistakes, and increases the probability for mission accomplishment. And when an organization's future, and the future of its customers and stakeholders, depends on mission accomplishment, true leaders can do nothing less.

It was just after midnight on 11 February 1997 when the whoopee alarm sounded at the Quillayute River Station in La Push, Washington. The Coast Guard performs nearly one hundred rescues each year at this isolated post on the Pacific coast where winds routinely exceed seventy five to one hundred miles per hour and waves reach heights of more than two stories. This night a sailboat had been caught up in an unusually bad storm and was reported to be sinking west of James Island at the mouth of the river.

The four Coasties on duty (a second-class boatswain's mate, age thirty-six; a petty officer third-class, age twenty-four; a twenty-two-year-old seaman; and a nineteen-year-old seaman apprentice barely four months out of Cape May) quickly jumped into their wetsuits and emergency vests, grabbed their safety belts, and launched a 44-foot Coast Guard steel-hulled boat to search for the sailboat. For some reason, they were not wearing safety helmets.

As the crew crossed a huge sandbar that separates the river from the open ocean, the boatswain's mate radioed in that the waves were approximately 15–16 feet and conditions were getting better. However, the storm quickly worsened. Waves as tall as 25–30 feet pitched the small boat high and low, and slammed mountains of water onto its deck. It became so dark that the crew could not see the bow of the boat and so loud that they could barely hear each other shouting only a few feet apart. A second Coast Guard boat started out as backup but was recalled due to the worsening conditions.

The first boat was then hit by a series of three huge waves. The first wave smashed the spotlight and bent the mast. The second wave slammed the boat from behind and engulfed it. When the boat righted itself, the windshield and cabin were destroyed, the mast was gone, and the boatswain's mate and the seaman were nowhere to be seen. Before the third wave hit, the petty officer third-class grabbed the seaman apprentice, whom he had seen disengage his safety belt, and told him to calm down and stay with the boat. Then he grabbed the radio and called in their position. The young seaman apprentice, however, knew that the radio was broken and that his shipmate had done that only to reassure him that things would be all right. But after the third wave crashed into the boat and sent it underwater, the petty officer was thrown overboard.

The young Coastie, now bleeding from the nose and right eye, clung to the wreckage of the boat and shot five distress flares into the air. Onshore, the second rescue boat saw the flares and immediately headed back out. This time, however, the seaman apprentice did not stay with what was left of the boat. He had shot the last two flares toward land and was able to gauge that the shore of James Island was not too far away. So he swam toward land and was able to climb a 50-foot jagged cliff and get away from the crashing waves. He then pulled a strobe light from his vest and turned it on.

A few minutes later, one of two rescue helicopters, also dispatched to aid the sailboat, spotted him. A high angle rescue team was called from the local sheriff's department. They reached the seaman apprentice, who was then hoisted up into the chopper and flown to the nearest medical facility. The second rescue boat was unable to find any part of the damaged Coast Guard boat, but the other helicopter was able to rescue the two people off the sinking sailboat.

Many hours later, the bodies of the three Coast Guardsmen were recovered. All three had died of head-related injuries. It turned out to be one of the worst accidents in Coast Guard search and rescue history. A four-month investigation determined that the boatswain's mate was both a hero and at fault. He had made serious errors in judgment, had misread the weather conditions, failed to adequately brief his crew, and failed to order safety helmets to be worn.

As a result of the accident, the Coast Guard implemented serious changes. It accelerated the replacement of the 44-foot steel-hulled boats with faster, safer, longer ones. It upgraded the safety hooks with newer, stronger models. It made stronger safety and training procedures mandatory. And it required that helmets be worn at all times in heavy seas.

All four members of the crew were awarded the Coast Guard Medal for bravery. At the public memorial service for the three fallen Coasties, hundreds of mourners cried openly. And the command master chief at the Quillayute River Station never quite got over the trauma. "I should have trained them more," he lamented. "I should have trained them more."

The Coast Guard on Leadership

Sponsor Continual Learning

- Leadership and learning go hand in hand.
- Part of constantly driving forward is getting knocked back a time or two.
- Create an organization where people are continually learning how to do their jobs better, where they are adapting to the changing times and creating new avenues to success.
- An organization imbued with continual learning helps eliminate mistakes and increase results.
- Teach people *how* to think, not what to think.
- Provide basic skills training and preparation early in the career of employees.
- Afford opportunities for refresher classes over the course of an individual's career.
- When new expertise is needed, rather than bringing in new people, first transform those who are already there.
- Adopt and employ new technology as the times change.
- Encourage people in the organization to always be thinking about improving and refining processes.
- Rely heavily on learning by doing. Put your people in the field and let them learn through trial and experience.
- The field is the greatest classroom and on-the-job experience is the greatest teacher.
- Perform in-depth post-mortem studies. Investigate yourself, even when it hurts, and broadcast the lessons learned.

Chapter 15

Spotlight Excellence

It is the duty of all responsible leaders, throughout every level in the organization, to foster appropriate formal recognition.

—Coast Guard standing order

Recognizing people for their achievements meets an important human need. It tells people that their *work* is valued by the organization and, more importantly, that *they* are valued by the organization.

When Buddy, a lieutenant commander, was assigned as skipper of the USCGC *Steadfast,* he resolved to put in practice all he had learned about leadership and the Quality Management process. Before he even showed up on site at Station San Francisco, he reviewed the history of his new ship, a 210-foot medium-endurance cutter with a crew of seventy-five. In the 1970s and 1980s, Buddy learned, it had been home-ported in St. Petersburg, Florida, and was renowned for effectiveness in drug interdiction. The *Steadfast*, it turned out, was one of only two cutters in the entire Coast Guard to have earned a Gold Marijuana Leaf, which signified the seizure of more than one million pounds of marijuana. Drug lords had nicknamed the ship "The White Shark" because it was so aggressive in seizing drugs coming out of Colombia. Buddy also ran across an old sketch of a shark with the *Steadfast's* name carefully printed inside, probably drawn by a former crew member.

When Buddy arrived on scene, he gave every crew member a tee-shirt and a sweatshirt with the sketch (now a logo) on it. He also had the logo stenciled on the side of the ship. Then he initiated a series of meetings that began an ongoing process of involvement and participation for all members of the crew. He wanted everybody to feel they were a part of the team, so nobody was left out. To develop a strategic plan, Buddy guided the discussions by utilizing criteria for winning the Malcolm Baldridge Award for excellence in Quality Management. He asked the following questions and received the following answers:

- *What is our core purpose?*
- We are a multi-mission cutter now and in the future. Our core purpose is tied to the Coast Guard's vision, values, and missions.
- *What exactly do we do?*
- Eighty-five percent of our work is in law enforcement—half in fisheries law enforcement, the other half in maritime customs enforcement. Fifteen percent is divided between search and rescue, military exercises, and public affairs.
- *What resources do we control?*
- We are on a 210-foot cutter. We have seventy-five crew members. We have a helicopter on our back and two small boats. And we have operating funds.
- *Who are our customers?*
- We are an instrument of the U.S. Coast Guard intended to serve the public. But we do not solicit requests from the public. We work for a tactical commander who deploys us to meet certain goals that originate from our headquarters.

- *What are our process requirements?*
- We have standards of conduct when we interface with the public. We are professional and courteous at all times. We are smart about our business. We produce morning reports, intelligence sightings reports, and so forth. We interface with other organizations, but we don't work for them.

With those questions answered, Buddy led his crew through the development of a strategic plan that had to have these four main ingredients:

- Simple—it had to fit on one sheet of paper.
- Realistic—it had to be achievable.
- Meaningful—it had to have a clear purpose and relate directly to the crew.
- Engaging—it had to motivate and inspire.

In a nutshell, the strategic plan stated: "The *Steadfast* must be able to accomplish a broad spectrum of activities, including detection, surveillance, inspection, enforcement, and response. The *Steadfast* will have unit readiness. The crew must have the right tools, equipment, and supplies on hand. The crew has to be skilled, knowledgeable, confident, and motivated to perform their jobs. The *Steadfast* crew will do the job with pride and professionalism, and in concert with the Coast Guard's core values of Honor, Respect, and Devotion to Duty."

After the plan was completed, Buddy took care to live by it. He felt that if he didn't follow through, neither would the crew. After all, the crew takes on the behavior of the skipper. In addition, he maintained constant communication and contact with everybody, holding frequent small group meetings all over the ship. Finally, he empowered his crew to act on their own. This act alone earned him tremendous respect. It gave the crew an opportunity to perform on their own, but also showed how much their CO trusted them. But even though Buddy stayed a step or two back, he also watched closely and stayed abreast of everything they were doing. He did not want them to fail.

The *Steadfast* crew came up with strategic initiatives on their own. Morale and crew satisfaction were at the highest levels. And the work output was tremendous. Within the next six months, the *Steadfast* had two multi-ton cocaine seizures, more than one hundred fishery and customs boardings, and numerous multi-unit search and rescue calls.

Buddy just stood back and let it happen. The crew was trained, prepared, motivated, inspired, and oriented toward action. The entire process gave them confidence in themselves. And the *Steadfast* won the Commandant's Quality Award. It was the first time an entire crew had received the award.

When people in the Coast Guard do things really well, the organization recognizes, rewards, and shines a spotlight on them for all to see. In the case of the *Steadfast,* its commanding officer was invited to make a formal presentation at the Coast Guard Flag Conference (held twice a year for all admirals). While there, Buddy was not only a key speaker, he was given the opportunity to interact via informal discussions with flag officers from across the United States. Every admiral was able to see that Buddy had actually put to practical use the theoretical management approach called Total Quality Management (TQM) and, in so doing, had shown it to be an efficient tool to imbue leadership throughout an organization. And the admirals were duly impressed. They took back to their home stations copies of the lieutenant commander's presentation and talked up the *Steadfast*'s example. In effect, then, the story of the *Steadfast* became a how-to model for more effective leadership on cutters.

The practice of giving out appropriate awards and recognition is viewed in the Coast Guard as an important leadership responsibility. Officers and chiefs are advised to "aggressively seek recognition opportunities for your subordinates" so that "rewards become a hallmark of our service." The Coast Guard has a comprehensive recognition system that has become an important part of the culture of the organization.

There are individual and team awards, local, regional, and national. There are awards for operational excellence, sustained excellence, quality, leadership, heroism, and valor. Even Coast Guard ships and aircraft receive recognition that symbolizes campaigns and achievements. Many cutters, for instance, can be seen sporting emblems on their bows: a gold leaf for a major marijuana seizure, a snowflake for a significant cocaine bust, a raft for a Cuban or Haitian mass migration, and so forth.

Because there are various levels of excellence, there are also various levels of awards. Informal recognition, for instance, acknowledges individuals, groups, or teams for achieving specific goals or completing special projects. It occurs more frequently than more formal awards and medals, and is usually accompanied by certificates of appreciation, plaques, mementos, or other items whose cost is under a hundred dollars. Supervisors can nominate individual subordinates, peers can nominate peers, and the awards are presented by supervisors and commanding officers.

Just about every Coast Guard unit selects a Sailor of the Quarter. Most enlisted personnel are eligible to be nominated. Appropriate gifts may be purchased with morale committee funds. And every winner becomes an automatic candidate for Sailor of the Year. Personnel often receive "Bravo Zulu!" ("Well Done!") letters of recognition from their commanding officers in the event of multiple SARs, unusually large workloads over a short period of time, or other special achievements.

The Coast Guard also has a formal awards program that is designed to recognize individual, team, or unit acts of heroism, valor, meritorious achievement, or meritorious service above and beyond the call of duty. This program is taken most seriously; "it is the duty of all responsible leaders, throughout every level in the organization, to foster appropriate formal recognition" for members of their team. These awards are usually presented by flag officers in formal ceremonies and consist of medals, ribbons, bars, certificates, and/or citations. The highest awards are the Coast Guard Medal, the Meritorious Service Medal, and the Gold and Silver Life-Saving Medals. Equivalent high-level aviation awards include the Distinguished Flying Cross and the Air Medal. There is, of course, a series of lower level awards, such as the Commendation Medal, the Achievement Medal, the Commandant's Letter of Commendation, and various Unit and Meritorious Commendations. A variety of independent organizations, such as the Coast Guard Foundation, also sponsor very prestigious annual and regional awards for Coast Guard people across the nation. A system of awards also exists for civilian employees and the Coast Guard Auxiliary.

Essential to the formal recognition program is the element of timeliness. Because the meaningfulness of an award decreases if it is not presented soon after the act or time of service being recognized, submission of recommendations for decorations and awards must be initiated in a prompt manner. Moreover, as one Coastie notes, "It is a bad practice to dole out awards to everyone as going away presents because it diminishes the value of the award to people who really deserve it."

The quality of being deserved is a key element of formal recognition. Not everyone receives recognition and awards are not given away easily, for one very important reason: The troops know who the top performers are, who really merits an award and who doesn't. It behooves leaders, then, to make sure that recognitions accurately reflect performance. Otherwise, there will be talk behind the scenes. "Hey, did you hear that the CO gave that guy a medal!" people will say. "Heck, that guy didn't deserve any award, much less a medal!" Giving awards out too frequently or presenting them to undeserving people can destroy the credibility of the leader as well as the integrity of the entire system.

Shining the spotlight on good performers by presenting them with awards is a fairly common leadership tool. But actually weaving the recognition system into the fabric of the organization is something else again. The Coast Guard does so in two notable ways.

First, awards have an effect on promotion and advancement. Enlisted personnel are given points toward promotion for some awards. The more prestigious the award, the more points given. Officers do not receive points if presented with medals, but awards are certainly noted and attached to their records. So, for both officers and enlisted personnel, awards become one of many factors taken into account for transfers, special assignments, and promotions. The recognition system is an effective tool for motivating employees. More than that, though, it is a key part of the Coast Guard's three-step cycle of achievement: (1) set standards; (2) hold people accountable to obtain results; (3) recognize and reward them when they perform with excellence. Additionally, Coast Guard personnel are required to wear some medals and the ribbons that accompany awards on uniforms. And they must be worn in a certain order, from highest to lowest. They are part of every individual's uniform, similar to the insignia that designate rank. Why would the Coast Guard make medals and awards part of their uniforms? Military tradition is certainly a factor. Soldiers and sailors have been wearing commendations for centuries. But there is a deeper reason lying beneath the surface of military tradition: The good work performed by members of the Coast Guard becomes part of who they are. Where they've been, what they've done, what they've earned are all part of who they are as people, not just employees. So their awards are made part of their uniforms, signifying to all their backgrounds, their character, and their courage. Many Coasties wear only three awards on their uniforms, the minimum requirement. Others wear them all, whether three or twenty-three. All wear them proudly. In this manner, the awards system becomes a visible display of pride in both individuals and the organization as a whole. And every leader knows that pride is a most important motivating factor in any organization.

By spotlighting excellence with awards and recognition, the Coast Guard is able to instill five key underlying principles that benefit the entire organization:

1. Pride. People take a lot of personal pride in receiving awards, both individually and in teams. Organizational pride serves as a bonding experience. Emblems of cutters and aircraft, for example, evoke memories of arduous missions involving sacrifice, dedication, and achievement. People are proud to serve on a cutter with such a history and proud to serve in an organization with such a cutter.

2. Esprit de corps. Awards and recognition contribute dramatically to elevating group spirit and honor in performing the organization's missions. They also bring to bear the time-honored military tradition of acknowledging heroism, valor, and duty above and beyond the call.

3. High morale. Recognizing people for their achievements meets an important human need. It tells people that their work is valued by the organization and, more important, that they are valued by the organization. People need positive feedback. When it is received, it makes a significant difference in their outlook on the job. Also, when people feel valued, they want to remain part of the organization. Therefore, an effective awards and recognition program is an important tool for retention.

4. Positive role modeling. Spotlighting individual and group acts of excellence provides real-life examples of what the organization considers excellent work. If people do not understand exactly what excellence is, then the entire organization may evolve into a group of mediocre performers.

5. <u>Inspiration and motivation to achieve</u>. A simple act of heroism, bravery, or kindness often inspires similar acts from other members of the organization. Shipmates may inspire shipmates. Pilots may inspire rescue swimmers. And when an organization spotlights and publicizes excellence on a broad basis, people from one part of the organization may well inspire people from another part.

In many business corporations, good work may be rewarded with a cash bonus or stock option. But few people know when someone is given such a reward because the news is almost always held confidential. But in the U.S. Coast Guard, everybody knows when an award is given and who has received it. Recognition is almost always presented in a group setting with members of the team present. When major awards are given, the Coast Guard showcases them in magazines and speeches, and they are routinely written up and placed on the organization's Web site for everyone in the public domain to take note.

It demonstrates to the American public that in the U.S. Coast Guard, there is, indeed, a hero around every corner. But even heroes need day-to-day recognition to perform at consistently high levels. People value personalized, unexpected praise from their supervisors or from the people they serve. A congratulatory handshake or a warm smile can go a long way. Some leaders give out Coast Guard coins on the spur of the moment. One admiral at Coast Guard headquarters on Buzzard's Point in Washington, D.C., hands out "Buzzard Bucks" that serve as "a note of thanks for a job well done."

But for people in the Coast Guard, where the ethos is public service, compassion, and "others above self," a kind word from the people they serve is perhaps the most valued reward of all. Nothing, absolutely nothing, will go further with a Coastie than a simple thank-you from an American citizen.

The following message was posted on the electronic bulletin board of a Coast Guard Air Station on the West Coast:

The Greatest Christmas Gift a Coastie Could Get
On December 23rd, I was in a store, in line, when I noticed a big burly

fisherman looking down at me. I looked over to him and he said: "You look half tough enough to be one of them Navy Seal guys."

I laughed and said, "Only half tough enough. That's why I'm a rescue swimmer in the Coast Guard."

He looked at me in silence and his eyes filled up with tears. As they rolled down his face, he put his hand out for me to shake. I shook his hand, and he said: "It's because of you guys that I'm here this Christmas to be around for my family. Thank you. Thank you. God bless you guys."

I wanted so much to ask him a thousand questions, but instead I left it alone and simply said: "You're welcome. Merry Christmas."

I walked out of the store with a huge lump in my throat thinking how proud I am to be in the Coast Guard. Sometimes I get frustrated with things in the Coast Guard, but I started thinking of the team effort it took to bring that fisherman home alive to his family. What it takes to keep our planes flying and training up.

I just wanted to pass this story on to all aviation, because that "thank you" was to all of us. And I believe that's better than any DFC or medal you'll ever be awarded.

Happy New Year.

The Coast Guard on Leadership

Spotlight Excellence

- When people do things really well, praise them, publicize their work, and see that others learn form their example.
- Advise leaders to aggressively seek recognition opportunities for their subordinates so that rewards become a hallmark of the organization.
- Create a comprehensive recognition system with both informal and formal awards for various levels of excellence.
- Reward both individual and team excellence.
- Give out awards in a timely, prompt manner, and make certain they are well deserved. Remember, the troops know who the top performers are.
- Tie recognitions and awards to promotion and advancement.
- Put in place this three-step cycle of achievement: (1) set standards; (2) hold people accountable to obtain results; (3) recognize and reward them when they perform with excellence.
- Remember, good work performed by members of the team becomes part of who they are.
- By spotlighting excellence with awards and recognition, endeavor to instill these five principles that will benefit your entire organization:
    1. Pride
    2. Esprit de corps
    3. High morale
    4. Positive role modeling
    5. Inspiration and motivation to achieve.
- Even heroes often need day-to-day recognition to perform at consistently high levels.
- A congratulatory handshake, a warm smile, or a simple thank-you can go a long way toward making people feel appreciated.

Chapter 16

Honor History and Tradition

I am proud to be a United States Coast Guardsman. I revere that long
line of expert seamen, who by their devotion to duty and sacrifice
of self, have made it possible for me to be a member of a
service honored and respected, in peace and war,
throughout the world.

—Opening of the Coast Guardsman's Creed

We walk in the footsteps of heroes past—and some
of those footprints are very fresh.

—Coast Guard Commandant

Joanna had flown all the way from Kodiak, Alaska, to Green Bay, Wisconsin.
She had rented a car and was driving northward through a scenic countryside of corn fields, farm houses, barns, and cows, about an hour from town.
"How can they build a ship here?" she wondered. "And how can we get it
out of here?"

It had been thirteen years since Joanna had graduated from the Coast Guard Academy. She was now thirty-four years old, a lieutenant commander, and on her way to the christening of a brand-new cutter. This would be her second command, since she had just participated in the decommissioning of the USCGC *Ironwood* in a formal and very emotional ceremony. When Joanna assumed command of the *Ironwood,* she first researched the ship's history and found that it had seen action in World War II, Korea, and Vietnam. Then she made certain that all members of the crew were aware of *Ironwood*'s background.

Now she was going to attend the christening of a new cutter, loaded with the latest innovations and modern technology. Her new ship was built by the Marinette Marine Corporation in Marinette, Wisconsin (located on the coast of Lake Michigan). The company was given the contract to build thirty ships largely because of the quality of its work force. Known for fine craftsmanship and for being ahead of schedule and under budget, Marinette was the perfect choice to give the Coast Guard the most bang for the buck and, thereby, be a good steward of the American taxpayer's dollar.

While Joanna's previous cutter had a long and distinguished history, her new cutter was going to begin with a huge legacy. It was to be christened in honor of the women who served in the Coast Guard during World War II. It would carry the name *SPAR,* which was the term used for the women's corps because, as an acronym of Semper Paratus (Always Ready), it symbolized their attitude and willingness to serve their country.

From 1942 to 1945, eleven thousand women enlisted and served in the Coast Guard. Most did not consider themselves any big deal. They were patriotic women who wanted to do their part and help end the war as soon as possible. Many, however, joined over their parents' objections. And when they first arrived in the Coast Guard, they were often met with something less than a warm reception by the male-dominated service. The women started out serving mostly in clerical positions. But their dedication and work ethic won over the doubters. More and more ratings opened up, which allowed the SPARs to serve as parachute riggers, boatswain's mates, gunner's mates, quartermasters, and air traffic controllers, and they also ran many of the highly classified LORAN (Long Range Aids to Navigation) stations. When the war ended, most of them simply went back home, married, and began families. The SPARs had done their part. They had served their country with pride and excellence, and they helped to lay a cornerstone for the future assimilation of women in the Coast Guard.

Now, on 12 August 2000, some fifty-five years later, many of the women were being honored for the first time. The Marinette Marina was packed that day. Thousands of local citizens showed up to pay their respects. When Joanna saw the ship, she was awestruck. It was up on blocks behind the podium and totally out of the water. With the entire hull visible, it looked startlingly huge and beautiful. This was the cutter she was going to command, a 225-foot buoy tender with all the latest technology. With forty crew members, her primary missions were to be aids to navigation, law enforcement, ice operations, search and rescue, and marine environmental protection.

The dignitaries on the podium included a U.S. senator, a U.S. representative, the Coast Guard chief of staff, the president and CEO of Marinette Marine, the senior reserve admiral in the Pacific area (where the cutter would be stationed), two of the SPARs, and the attorney general of the United States, Janet Reno. When the Coast Guard band struck up a patriotic tune, nearly a hundred SPARs marched in together. The women, now in their seventies and eighties, were all in uniform, blue skirts and white shirts. Many were wearing their original ties or hats. People present said the SPARs exhibited extraordinary vim and vigor. It was obvious they were proud, very proud. Many had brought along family members who had no idea that Grandma had served in the war.

After the SPARs took their seats of honor in the front rows, the speeches began. Everybody on the podium participated. When it was Joanna's turn, she was filled with pride and emotion. The legacy of the SPARs was a lot to live up to, and as the first woman CO of this ship, she was acutely aware that it was they who had paved the way for her.

"One of the privileges of command is having bells rung whenever I'm coming or going from a ship," she said near the end of her remarks. "Right now, it goes, 'Ding-ding. Now *Ironwood* arriving.' Before long, it'll be, 'Ding-

ding. Now *SPAR* arriving.' [applause] And it will sound like they're saying 'a SPAR is arriving.' And for a vicarious instant, I get to become one of you. I get to insert myself into the company of legends. [Joanna's voice was now breaking.] In christening this ship the *SPAR*, the Coast Guard salutes you for undertaking an adventure when your country needed you most. I thank you for establishing the vital beachhead in the battle for a woman's right to serve in uniform. When I hear those bells and the words 'Now *SPAR* arriving,' I will always think of you."

After all the remarks, Attorney General Janet Reno whacked the ship with a bottle of champagne, and the USCGC *SPAR* slid sideways into the water. Horns sounded, the band played, and camera shutters clicked. People cheered wildly. And many of the SPARs wept openly. It was a beautiful moment.

The United States Coast Guard has a glorious history of more than two centuries of ships, battles, and rescues. And there are countless Coast Guard heroes, as well. Heroes who made personal sacrifices, who fought with courage in times of war and peace, who persevered in the face of extraordinary hardship and danger in making rescues or enforcing the nation's laws. Many of them are etched in the granite of Coast Guard lore and tradition: Hopely Yeaton, Joshua James, Sumner Kimball, Harriet Lane, Elmer Stone, Richard Etheridge, Ida Lewis, John Midgett, David Jarvis, and Pappy Patterson, to name a few. And for every famous hero, there are thousands of anonymous men and women who performed heroically and yet never received or sought formal recognition.

The Coast Guard has served in every military engagement in which the nation has been involved, including the War of 1812, the Civil War, the Spanish-American War, World War I, World War II, Korea, Vietnam, the Persian Gulf, and Iraq. And Coasties have always been there in peacetime, too, enforcing the law during Prohibition and the Cuban and Haitian mass migrations, responding to environmental disasters such as Hurricane Andrew in Florida and the Exxon *Valdez* oil spill in Alaska, and participating in search and recovery operations for the crashes of TWA 800 and the *Challenger* and *Columbia* space shuttles.

Coast Guard history and tradition is part of the fabric of the organization.

New recruits learn the lore early on. In fact, they are surrounded by it. At Cape May and the Academy, the streets and buildings are named after Coast Guard heroes. The core values of Honor, Respect, and Devotion to Duty are everywhere, on walls, on floors, on note pads. Part of the curriculum includes a heavy dose of history in order to provide the new recruits and cadets with an understanding of what the Coast Guard is and what it does. Instructors make certain everybody knows what the traditions are, who the people were who came before them, and who made it possible for them to serve in the Coast Guard.

Everyone learns, for example, the World War II story of twenty-two-year-old Signalman First-Class Douglas Munro. On 27 September 1942, Munro was credited with saving the lives of five hundred beleaguered Marines during a daring evacuation at Point Cruz, Guadalcanal, in the South Pacific. In charge of ten landing boats that day, he had volunteered to lead the evacuation. Near the end of the mission, enemy fire increased dramatically, and in order to save lives, Munro placed his craft as a shield between the beachhead and the men in the water. He was killed just as the last few Marines were getting into the boats. For his heroism, Douglas Munro was posthumously awarded the Congressional Medal of Honor.

Cadets and recruits are also exposed directly to Coast Guard veterans such as Marvin Perrett, who drove one of the Higgins boats that landed U.S. troops at Normandy on D-Day, 6 June 1944. Mr. Perrett will often show up at lectures wearing the original dungaree uniform and helmet he had on when he transported the Marines to Utah Beach. He will give a talk about his experiences and then stick around to talk informally with the students.

Like Mr. Perrett, many Coast Guard veterans, both retired and active, become company mentors at Cape May and the Academy. This personal interaction not only validates and echoes what the company commanders are teaching, it provides a tangible link to the past, to the history and tradition of the organization.

And when many of the recruits and cadets graduate, they have tears in their eyes. The tears come not so much from having made it through the nine weeks of boot camp or the four years at the Academy, but more from the recognition that they are now formally members of a great organization. They have learned about the people who came before them and of the extraordinarily heroic things they did. And now it is their turn to carry the torch, to uphold the tradition, to preserve, protect, and defend the nation.

Graduation, however, is not the end of the Coast Guard's focus on history and tradition. It is just the beginning. Everywhere Coasties go, for the rest of their careers, they are surrounded by constant reminders of the past. Just as at Cape May and the Academy, buildings and streets at the Yorktown and Petaluma Training Centers are named after Coast Guard heroes.

Many ships honor heroes, as well. The Hero class of high-endurance cutters sport such names as *Munro, Jarvis,* and *Midgett.* Many buoy tenders are named after Coast Guard legends. The *Harry Claiborne* stationed in Galveston, Texas, for instance, was named in honor of the keeper of the Point Bolivar Lighthouse, whose heroism saved the lives of hundreds of people during the great hurricane of 1900, which destroyed most of the city of Galveston. A Polar Icebreaker, the *Healy,* is named in honor of Captain Michael A. Healy, the sole representative of U.S. legal authority in Alaska and its coastal waters for most of the latter part of the nineteenth century.

Ships and office buildings have pictures on the walls of Coast Guard heroes, core values, and traditions. The USCGC *SPAR,* for instance, has a framed original World War II recruitment poster and numerous mementos and pictures of the first women who served in the Coast Guard. Furthermore, a great many organization-wide awards are named after inspirational men and women who have served with distinction.

Then there are the countless traditional ceremonies that occur throughout the Coast Guard on a regular basis. They serve as a constant reminder of the lore and history of the organization. They include the chief's call to initiation, the change of command, the christening and commissioning of cutters, promotion ceremonies, and awards ceremonies. From the swearing-in ceremony to the retirement ceremony to the final farewell at a Coastie's funeral, once a member of the Coast Guard, always a member of the Coast Guard. The organization is, in virtually every sense of the word, a family.

Honoring history and tradition not only binds the past to the present, it provides a link to the future. That, in turn, instills several key elements that benefit any organization, large or small, public or private:

1. Gives purpose and meaning. People join an organization, in part,
   because of what it does, what it means, and what it stands for. In the
   Coast Guard, members serve not for the money, but for the missions
   and for their country. Everybody desires to be part of something bigger.

It's part of a fundamental human need. People want to do something that is meaningful, that has a purpose, that provides a reason for living.

2. Provides a sense of pride. An understanding of past greatness gives people a sense of pride. The Coast Guard's history and tradition is the organization's foundation, its rock. "I am proud to be a United States Coast Guardsman," begins the Coast Guardsman's Creed. "I revere that long line of expert seamen, who by their devotion to duty and sacrifice of self, have made it possible for me to be a member of a service honored and respected, in peace and war, throughout the world."

3. Fortifies long-term decision making. Executives often make decisions based on the moment, based on current events. A respect for history and tradition makes leaders think about the future. "What will the impact of this decision be on the future of the organization?" they will ask themselves. "Let's be sure that we do not do anything to bring dishonor on those who came before us."

4. Enhances strength and courage. Strength and courage are drawn from the great heroes who have come before. Their stories provide tangible examples of past success. No matter how difficult the situation in which current members may find themselves, they know that someone experienced something similar or worse before, and they pulled through. Additionally, no one wants to let down the organization's past heroes. Rather, they want to build on the legacy. That desire breeds strength, sustenance and courage in any given situation.

5. Motivates and inspires. When people are part of a great organization that formally documents its history, they know that their fingerprints will be on everything they do. There is no question about it, they will be judged by future leaders. That recognition motivates and inspires people to do a better job because no one wants to be looked upon in a negative light. No one wants to dishonor the memory of heroes past. A common vow in the Coast Guard is: "Nothing that tarnishes our history or tradition will happen on my watch."

Solid history and tradition in an organization serves as a foundation upon which everything else rests. For the U.S. Coast Guard, it's the long blue line, the core values of Honor, Respect, and Devotion to Duty, and an anchor that dates back to the dawn of the nation itself, to the U.S. Constitution, to Alexander Hamilton, and to other great champions of character and action.

"Heroic Coasties have made their mark in every mission area and every era of our service," remarked one former Commandant of the Coast Guard. "We are the heirs of their legacy. We walk in the footsteps of heroes past, and some of those footprints are very fresh. Today we have helicopter crews rescuing thirty-four people from a sinking cruise ship more than two hundred miles east of North Carolina. Today we have marine safety professionals keeping a major oil spill in Louisiana from becoming an environmental catastrophe. Today we have small boat crews saving the lives of heart attack victims off the coast of New Jersey. We are, indeed, upholding the legacy of our service. Coast Guard heroes of the future will walk not only in the footsteps of heroes past, but in the footsteps of heroes present."

That, in essence, is the promise of an organization with a great history, with great tradition: That however good it was, however good it is now, it has a chance to be even better.

It's a promise that the best days of the Coast Guard are still ahead. That the organization has not yet experienced its finest hour. That the best is yet to be.

_____

When Alexander Hamilton founded the Revenue-Marine in 1790, his intent was to create "a strong right arm" for the new nation—an organization specifically designed to preserve, protect, and defend the Constitution of the United States of America. Over more than two centuries, that fledgling organization has grown and evolved into the institution that is today known as the United States Coast Guard. With every reorganization, every adjustment, and every modification, Alexander Hamilton's original intent was the basis for change. As a result, the missions of the modern-day Coast Guard have a direct relationship with the reasons listed in the preamble to the U. S. Constitution as to why the nation was founded in the first place.

Preamble to the Constitution of the United States of America

"We the people of the United States, in order to form a more perfect union, establish justice, insure domestic tranquility, provide for the common defense, promote the general welfare, and secure the blessings of liberty to ourselves and our posterity, do ordain and establish this Constitution of the United States of America."

United States Coast Guard Missions *as related to the* Preamble of the Constitution of the United States of America

"We the people of the United States, in order to form a more perfect union ...,

establish justice,
  - **Maritime Law Enforcement**

insure domestic tranquility,
  - **Homeland Security**
  - **Port Safety and Security**
  - **Environmental Response**

provide for the common defense,
  - **Defense Operations**

promote the general welfare,
  - **Search and Rescue**
  - **Aids to Navigation**
  - **Boating Safety**
  - **Maritime Inspection**
  - **Maritime Science**
  - **Marine Licensing**

and secure the blessings of liberty to ourselves and our posterity,
  - **Waterways Management**
  - **Ice Operations**

... do ordain and establish this Constitution of the United States of America."

THE COAST GUARD ON LEADERSHIP

Honor History and Tradition

- Make history and tradition part of the fabric of your organization.
- Teach new people the lore early on. Include in your curriculum a heavy dose of history.
- During training, bring in mentors and veterans for personal interaction with students. Doing so will provide a tangible link to the past.
- Make sure that employees are surrounded with visible reminders of the past. Name awards, buildings, and other sites after past heroes.
- Encourage people to uphold the traditions of the past and not to let down those who built what they now enjoy.
- Make your organization like a family in every sense of the word.
- Honoring history and tradition instills several elements that benefit any organization:
    1. Gives purpose and tradition
    2. Provides a sense of pride
    3. Fortifies long-term decision making
    4. Enhances strength and character
    5. Motivates and inspires.
- Solid history and tradition in an organization serves as a foundation upon which everything else rests.
- The promise of an organization with a great history and great tradition is that however good it was, however good it is now, it has a chance to be even better.

Epilogue

On Tuesday morning, 11 September 2001, Ed, the director of the local Coast Guard Auxiliary, was in his office at Battery Park on the southern tip of Manhattan, five blocks from the World Trade Center. He had just opened his windows to enjoy the cool autumn breeze and was sitting at his computer looking out toward the Statue of Liberty and a calm Hudson Bay. At exactly 8:45 A.M., he heard a loud bang and a scream. The commander's first thought was that the Staten Island ferry had been in an accident at its nearby dock. But someone across the hall screamed that a plane had hit one of the World Trade Center towers. Ed rushed out of his office to the opposite window, looked up, and saw a ball of flames on the north tower. "My God!" he thought, "a small plane or sightseeing helicopter must have gotten too close. Probably a terrible accident."

Meanwhile, the SAR alarm sounded across the harbor at Coast Guard Station New York and, within five minutes, a 41-foot small boat with three young Coasties was headed toward Battery Park. In charge of the boat was a twenty-year-old petty officer third-class named Carlos who had completed his qualifications to be a coxswain only two weeks earlier. He had never before been in charge of a small boat, and this was his first search and rescue case. The only thing he had been told was that a plane had apparently hit one of the twin towers and that he was to proceed across the harbor to see if the Coast Guard might render any assistance.

At 9:03 A.M., and now within only a few hundred yards of Battery Park, one of the crew yelled, "Hey, Carlos, do you hear that?" They looked up and saw a United Airlines passenger jet flying a few hundred feet above their heads. It was so low that all three men ducked reflexively. Then they watched in disbelief as the plane flew directly into the south tower of the World Trade Center and exploded into a massive fireball. It was unbelievable, unthinkable. Communications on the small boat instantly went dead. Carlos and his crew could not be reached, nor could they call out. Both towers were now on fire, and for the moment, the three young people were in charge of the only Coast Guard vessel in New York Harbor.

Up at Air Station Cape Cod in Massachusetts, the commanding officer was carefully monitoring the situation in New York City. Because his unit housed two heavy-duty search and rescue Sikorski helicopters, he knew there could be a call any minute to dispatch them to the scene. Upon hearing that the first tower had been hit, the captain had ordered the helicopters to stand by for action. But when he saw the airliner crash into the second tower live on television, he did not wait for a call. The CO immediately gave the order for his pilots to saddle up and get down there.

By 9:10 A.M., the two Sikorski helicopters had taken off from Cape Cod, each with a four-person crew consisting of a pilot, copilot, navigator, and rescue swimmer. Along the way, the teams made plans for basket lifts off the towers. They were going to put the rescue swimmers in the basket, lower them to the roofs, and pick up as many people as they could. If people weren't on the roofs, they would attempt rescues from the windows of the upper floors. One thing they knew for certain, the Coast Guard was the only service that had this kind of rescue capability, and they were the guys who had to make it happen. Operational speed for the Sikorskis is normally 130 knots, but the pilots pushed it up to 157 knots, figuring at that speed they could make it to lower Manhattan in less than an hour.

Much of the senior Coast Guard leadership was not at Activities New York (Marine Safety Office) on Staten Island that morning. They were traveling by train to headquarters in Washington, D.C., for an important meeting. The captain of the port (COTP) was out, as were four other senior officers. The Coast Guard personnel present were monitoring events in lower Manhattan with the Vessel Traffic Service's closed-circuit television system. But when the plane hit the second tower, their camera feeds were knocked out. The deputy commander, a captain, acted without hesitation and immediately ordered New York Harbor closed. Utilizing VHF channel 16, the Operations Center radioed out to all vessel pilots: "The captain of the port has closed the port of New York. No vessels may enter or move without his permission." The Coast Guard also started sending out an Urgent Mariner Information Broadcast (UMIB) relating more detailed information and the current status of events. A list was compiled of all known vessels currently in the harbor, and preparations began for a command center briefing. The procedures used to close the harbor were identical to those the Coast Guard uses when, for example, a hurricane is approaching or a major oil spill has occurred. By now it was obvious that the New York City was under a terrorist attack. Port security was of paramount concern.

Back in the office at Battery Park, rumors ran rampant that bombs were exploding all over lower Manhattan. Being only five blocks from the twin towers, many people began to panic. Some became hysterical. And there was an awful lot of screaming. Ed realized that, as a lieutenant commander, he was the ranking officer in the building, so he took charge. After the first plane hit, he had held an all hands meeting and encouraged everyone to remain calm and to call their families and tell them they were okay. When the second plane hit, however, he immediately summoned all the chiefs and civilian supervisors. "Communications are down," he said. "The phone systems run through the World Trade Center. We have to secure the building. Shut all the windows, lock the doors, and clear the roof. Have people put the blinds down and stay away from the windows. If there are more explosions, we don't want people injured by flying glass."

Out on the water, Carlos and the two members of his crew conferred. This had to be a terrorist attack, they concluded. Even though they did not have orders and could not be contacted, they were certain the COTP would shut down the harbor. They also knew that people were going to be evacuating the twin towers. Civilians were already starting to show up at the piers. Collectively, the team decided the best thing to do was to begin organizing the tugs, ferries, and other vessels that were starting to congregate haphazardly around Battery Park.

"Okay," said Carlos. "Let's get moving."

At 9:40 A.M., the Federal Aviation Administration halted all flight operations at all airports in the United States. It was the first time in U.S. history that had been done. All international flights were diverted to Canada. Existing flights were ordered out of the air. And the FAA began a tabulated list to account for every single airplane that had taken off from a major airport.

The Commandant of the Coast Guard had scrambled his senior staff together when word of the first tower strike reached him. The team was monitoring events in his office when the second tower was hit.

"One plane hitting the World Trade Center may be an accident," said one of the admirals. "But two times in the same place—this was planned."

"Can't be accidental," agreed another. "Got to be a terrorist attack."

"First things first," said the Commandant. "Let's get hold of the Secretary and get his approval to call up the Reserves. Everybody agree."

"Yes."

"Absolutely."

Everyone knew that 70–80 percent of the nation's trade traveled through 361 major seaports, and action needed to be taken immediately to make certain they were secured from terrorist attacks. So the Commandant picked up the phone and called his boss, the Secretary of Transportation. (On 11 September 2001, the U.S. Coast Guard was part of the Department of Transportation.) The Secretary immediately granted the request because he knew that the main mission of the Coast Guard Reserve concerned port security. "I'll get the written approval to you right away," said the Secretary. "In the meantime, do what you have to do. If you need to reach me, I'll be in the Situation Room at the White House."

As soon as the Commandant hung up, he was told that his good friend, the Chief of Naval Operations, was holding. "Jim, I recognize the Coast Guard's lead role in the maritime security of the homeland," Admiral Vern Clark told the Commandant. "As you have always helped the Navy meet our national responsibilities overseas, the Navy is now standing by to help you. Just tell us what you need."

"Thank you, Vern," replied the Commandant. "I'll be getting back to you shortly."

Both phone calls were very brief. So within only a few minutes of deciding that increased port security would have to be an immediate course of action, the Coast Guard had the approval of the Secretary of Transportation and the unconditional support of the U.S. Navy.

A short time later, at 9:43 A.M., the Coast Guard building shuddered and shook from what felt like a sonic boom. "What the hell was that?" somebody shouted.

Phones immediately started ringing in the Commandant's office. "Sir, we're receiving reports that there was an explosion at the State Department or somewhere close to the White House," said an aide.

Within minutes, another aide ran in. "Sir, the Pentagon's been hit. A plane just flew into it. We can see it out of the west windows of the building across the river. There's a big cloud over it."

Orders were immediately issued to secure Buzzard's Point in case there were more terrorist attacks, and Coast Guard cutters were sent out to secure the Potomac River. The Commandant and his executive team then quickly placed a conference call to the Atlantic and Pacific area commanders in Virginia and California, respectively.

"Let's get focused on our captains of the port," said the Commandant. "We need them to make port security their number-one priority."

"Yes, sir," replied the area commanders, both three-star admirals. "We'll get right on it."

No sooner had the phone conversation ended than another of the Commandant's aides burst into the room. "Sir," he said, "we've just received word from the FAA that there is another hijacked airliner headed toward Washington."

At 10:05 A.M., the south tower of the World Trade Center (the second tower hit) collapsed onto the streets below. A massive cloud of cement dust, paper, and other debris filled the air and began to drift with the wind toward Battery Park. For two or three minutes, Ed could see absolutely nothing. But as the dust cloud began to settle, a mass of terrified people, running along the streets and coming out of the subway, came rushing toward the waterfront. Some were climbing along the sea wall, and many jumped into the water. Within a matter of minutes, a crowd of thousands packed Battery Park and the Staten Island Ferry Terminal. Many were having trouble breathing amid all the dust, grit, and debris. Coast Guard personnel in the building threw life jackets to those in the water, passed out towels and other cloth materials for people to put over their faces, and provided drinking water.

Meanwhile, members of the New York Coast Guard Auxiliary jumped into action. A retired comptroller on Staten Island rushed to his boat and took it straight to the nearest bridge seeking to stop any boat traffic going down the river. On the coast of New Jersey, the rear commodore for auxiliary activities north called up all flotilla boats and headed toward Sandy Hook to coordinate operations. A sales manager in New Rochelle walked into his boss's office and said: "They need me. I'm leaving." An investment banker in Mamaroneck sprinted out of his office without saying a word to anyone and raced to the nearby marina. A dentist in Brooklyn canceled all his appointments and went straight to his boat. All over the countryside, Coast Guard auxiliarists charged to the scene, or to a waterway or a bridge to help with security, or to offer their services at the nearest Coast Guard station.

Emergency chief's calls were convened nearly everywhere in the Coast Guard. On the cutters, in the air stations, at the small boat stations, in marine safety offices, at integrated support commands, wherever active duty members were stationed, Coast Guard chiefs got together to evaluate the situation, organize themselves, and take appropriate action. Security at bases and buildings was stepped up. All personnel were put on alert. And plans were drawn up with junior and senior officers to secure and protect ports, power plants, bridges, government buildings, and any other facility that might be at risk.

At the Activities New York Command Center, a briefing was held with Coast Guard and other government agency personnel. The deputy commander asked one of his junior officers, a lieutenant named M.D., to take a 41-foot small boat and "go out there, observe, and try to make it a safer operation."

"Yes, sir," he responded.

In the room was a New York harbor pilot who knew Lt. M.D. quite well. "Sir," he said, "the Pilot Boat *New York* has been prepped for a social function later tonight. It's all fueled and ready to go. It's just down the street from here and can be under way in ten minutes. I'd like to volunteer its services."

Over the years, the Coast Guard had built up a close relationship with the New York Harbor Pilots Association. The Coasties attended meetings, met people, and made certain that the pilots knew the Coast Guard was their friend. To become a harbor pilot, a candidate had to undertake a fourteen-year apprenticeship and learn to draw details of New York Harbor from rote memory. This man was not only offering the services of a 200-foot pilot boat, he was also offering considerable expertise and local knowledge of New York Harbor.

"Thanks, Andy," said the lieutenant. "We accept."

A Customs officer was also in the room and offered to provide transportation. "Hey, M.D.," he said, "I've got a car downstairs. Let me drive you guys over there."

"Okay, buddy. Let's go!"

On the way out the door, the lieutenant grabbed some large laminated charts of the harbor and a list of the vessels there. Then they all rushed outside, hopped in the Customs car and, with sirens blaring, sped eight blocks to the Sandy Hook Pilot's Station. A second car followed close behind with a senior chief and four enlisted Coasties who had volunteered for the operation. When they arrived, the crew of the *New York* had been alerted and were ready to depart. On the six-mile trip from Staten Island to Battery Park, Lt. M.D. got his team together, rolled out his maps, and did some planning. They looked at where casualties might be taken, where ambulances could be staged, where emergency supplies might be brought in, where the best evacuation points would be, and where to take people.

And they paused for a minute to listen to an emergency broadcast on the radio: "Any vessel that can help evacuate people from lower Manhattan, please proceed to Battery Park."

The pilots in the two Sikorski helicopters speeding down from Cape Cod received word that the south tower had collapsed, that there was nobody on the roof of the north tower, and that people were breaking windows and, in some cases, jumping out. The teams knew that the wind was blowing out of the north and reasoned that they could use it to blow the basket toward the windows and pick people out that way. It was worth a shot, they felt. "We can do it," they said to each other. But when they reached Long Island, the FAA and the Air Force ordered both helicopters out of the air. Upon landing, the pilots charged into the air traffic control tower and begged to be allowed to go into lower Manhattan and attempt some rescues. "It's too dangerous," they were told. "The government has ordered everything out of the air, period."

At 10:10 A.M., news wires flashed word that a fourth passenger airliner had crashed in the countryside of Somerset County, Pennsylvania, southeast of Pittsburgh. It had taken off from Newark, New Jersey, with a planned destination of San Francisco, but was apparently hijacked and headed for a target in Washington, D.C. It was believed the passengers on board fought the terrorists before the plane went down.

Back in New York Harbor, Carlos and his crew on the Coast Guard small boat were laboring diligently on the water to make organization out of chaos. They had taken control of the boats in the area and were directing ferries where to pick up people. But after the emergency radio request for help went out, a virtual armada of tugs, ferries, and boats of every description—hundreds of them—descended upon Battery Park and tried to get to any available site to pick up people. This was the frenzied scene that Lt. M.D. and the fourteen-person crew of the pilot boat *New York* observed when they arrived on the scene. They were just coming up on the Battery and surveying the situation when a thunderous quaking rumble began. Lt. M.D. looked up and saw the remaining World Trade Center tower collapsing onto itself from the top down, the floors above slamming onto each successive floor below until the structure disappeared into an enormous cloud of debris, dust, and smoke.

Again, the unthinkable had happened. Both towers of the World Trade Center had collapsed. Tens of thousands of panic-stricken citizens quickly descended on the Staten Island Ferry Terminal and Battery Park. Many were covered head to toe in dust. There was screaming, wailing, and mass confusion. And the only way out of this part of lower Manhattan was by water. The young Coast Guard lieutenant now had a mass evacuation staring him square in the face. Tens of thousands, perhaps hundreds of thousands of people needed help. But there was no formal procedure designed to handle an operation of this magnitude. He was going to have to improvise and do the best he could.

The first thing Lt. M.D. did was to run the Coast Guard flag up the mast of the *New York*. After realizing that both primary and secondary communications were down (because all the communications cables ran through the World Trade Center) he got on a VHF hand-held radio and started making broadcasts: "This is the United States Coast Guard aboard the pilot vessel," he said. "All vessels assisting with the evacuation please follow our directions so that we may coordinate this rescue operation in the most efficient manner."

The lieutenant next dropped a Coastie off at Pier 11 to coordinate the boarding of people. He also ordered the removal of all tugboats from the area because the pier was designed for ferries. Tugboats and other vessels were moved down the line to more appropriate marshaling and docking areas, and on each, the lieutenant dropped off a Coastie or a harbor pilot crew member to coordinate activity. These moves, alone, started a more orderly and efficient process that showed immediate results. When people saw that things were proceeding in an orderly manner, their panic seemed to wane a bit. Interestingly, everybody followed the directions of the Coast Guard, civilians, boat pilots and crews, even members of the pilot boat. The young lieutenant had taken charge with unhesitating strength and confidence.

One of the vessels traveling between Jersey City, New Jersey, and North Cove, New York, reported to Lt. M.D. that numerous rescue people and supplies were massing on the Jersey City side of the Hudson. Food, water, medical equipment, doctors, EMTs, blankets, firefighters, members of the New Jersey National Guard, members of the Iron Workers, and a slew of other volunteers all were waiting for transportation into lower Manhattan to begin relief and rescue operations. Lt. M.D. immediately got on the radio and directed all volunteer vessels that wanted to help to proceed to Jersey City and bring all these supplies and rescue personnel to North Cove.

When the *New York* finally tied up at the sea wall outside North Cove, a group of New York firefighters reported that they were unable to get fuel to their water pump trucks. So the crew organized volunteers into a half-mile-long bucket brigade using water cooler bottles filled with diesel fuel from the *New York* and transported the fuel to the pump trucks. Later, an engineer from one of the tugboats said he thought he could fashion a fueling nozzle so that the firetrucks could be driven directly up to the pilot boat. Lt. M.D. authorized him to go ahead. And soon, there was a block-long line of firetrucks waiting in line to get fuel from the pilot boat.

Back at Battery Park, dozens of Auxiliary members showed up in Ed's office. "What are you doing here?" he asked in surprise. "We're here to help, sir," came the response. "We can answer phones, take care of paperwork, and anything else that will free you up to focus on rescue and evacuation efforts."

It was that way all over the New York coastal area, as members of the Coast Guard Auxiliary showed up without being asked. They came to Activities New York, Station Sandy Hook, Station Long Island, Station Eaton's Neck, Station Fire Island, every single Coast Guard station. And they did what they could to help. Mostly, they freed up the active duty Coast Guard members from paperwork and communications so the active duty personnel could concentrate on port security. But many also took responsibility for search and rescue operations as well as security in certain areas that could not be covered any other way. Volunteers all, the auxiliarists acted without being asked. They just did it.

Shortly before 11:30 A.M., American Airlines and United Airlines released news reports that each had experienced the loss of two aircraft. Up to this point, no one had known for certain which planes hit what targets, from where they originated, or to where they were headed.

American Airlines flight 11, a Boeing 767 flying from Boston to Los Angeles, had eighty-one passengers and eleven crew members on board. This plane hit the north tower of the World Trade Center.

United Airlines flight 175, flying from Boston to Los Angeles with fifty-six passengers and nine crew members on board, crashed into the World Trade Center's south tower.

American Airlines flight 77, a Boeing 757 en route from Dulles International Airport to Los Angeles, had fifty-eight passengers and six crew members on board. This is the plane that hit the Pentagon.

United Airlines flight 93, en route from Newark to San Francisco with thirty-eight passengers and seven crew members on board, crashed in Pennsylvania.

Evidence indicated that all four planes had been hijacked by terrorists. Each had obviously been carefully selected having had cross-country maximum loads of jet fuel.

Coast Guard officers were focusing on security around the entire nation. With ninety-five thousand miles of coastline, thousands of inland waterways and bridges, and hundreds of coastal refineries and power plants to look after, there was prioritizing, planning, and decisive action.

Orders were communicated via telephone, fax, e-mail, video conferencing, and personal conversation. At Puget Sound in the state of Washington, a Regional Incident Command was quickly established at the district office. Teams were maintained twenty-four hours a day. Small boats and cutters were called out in force and ongoing patrols established. In the Great Lakes, with more than fifteen hundred miles of international maritime border, nearly every large ship was stopped. In Cleveland, the Coast Guard worked with the neighboring Canadians to the north to make certain all borders were secure and all ships checked out. In Chicago, every nuclear plant, every water intake system, every major coastal facility was secured. In the Caribbean Sea, in the Gulf of Mexico, and in the Hawaiian Islands and Guam, every cruise ship was boarded, passenger manifests reviewed, and security precautions instituted.

Orders were also given to recall all Coast Guard cutters from extended deployments to provide increased port security. The *Bear* went from the Windward Passage off Cuba straight to Charleston Harbor. The *Forward* also shifted from Caribbean drug interdiction to patrols off the coast of Virginia. All Coast Guard helicopters and aircraft, usually relegated to SAR and drug interdiction missions, were directed to help in port security all around the country.

Reservists had begun to mobilize and were reporting for duty everywhere. And when the Commandant subsequently ordered the immediate call-up of the Coast Guard Auxiliary, he was told: "Sir, they're already out there. And not just in New York, but all over the country, Portland, Seattle, San Francisco, San Diego, Los Angeles, Miami, Houston, New Orleans, Charleston, you name it, they're already there.

"God bless them," responded the Commandant. "Send out the directive anyway. It'll give their activity official status."

Back at Battery Park in lower Manhattan, Ed had organized his staff and other auxiliarists. They loaded up vans with food, water, and ice, then drove to Ground Zero to aid New York firefighters and police. They went up Broadway where the street was covered with dust several inches deep. There also were millions of pieces of paper all over the place from the thousands of offices of people who worked in the twin towers every day. The scene was surreal: like a European combat zone during World War II, like a ghost town in the Old West.

On the edge of the World Trade Center, the vans pulled up next to Trinity Church and began handing out six-packs of water to firefighters. Ed looked to his left and was amazed that Trinity Church had not been damaged by the collapsed towers. He looked over at the tombstones in the graveyard at Trinity. They were covered with a foot of dust and ash. When Ed realized he was right next to Alexander Hamilton's grave, he paused to look at it and then nodded. He told himself they were doing the right thing. They were doing all they could.

On any given workday, one hundred eighty-six thousand people come and go to work in New York by ferry. By nightfall on 11 September 2001, between seven hundred fifty thousand and one million people had left lower Manhattan. Many had walked out over bridges—the Brooklyn Bridge, the Manhattan Bridge, the Williamsburg Bridge. Many hundreds of thousands had been evacuated by water.

At around midnight, eighty-year-old Lou was on guard near the Verrazano Narrows Bridge. A retired financial analyst, Lou had pulled his crew together (consisting of his wife, Trudy, and their friend, Delores) and reported to Station Sandy Hook shortly after the attacks. He had been asked by his flotilla commander to patrol the water near the bridge and be on the lookout for any suspicious vessels. No one knew whether or not there was going to be any more terrorist activity, or where it might come from or where it might be headed. Consequently, everybody was taking the situation extremely seriously.

At one point Lou wondered what he was going to do if an unauthorized vessel tried to get past him. His 32-foot cabin cruiser was loaded with all the latest technology—GPS, radar, you name it—but he did not have any guns. He decided he would first call in for help. Then he would ram the vessel with his own boat and try to disable it. He was not going to let *anything* get past him, no matter what.

On Wednesday morning, 12 September 2002, at Fort Eustis, Virginia, some one hundred men and women dressed in camouflage uniforms were packing their bags and seven tractor-trailer trucks with all the necessary gear to operate a small city for forty-five days. They were members of the Coast Guard Reserve assigned to a Port Security Unit (PSU). Mostly civilians, they had been called up to help relief efforts in New York City. They had just said goodbye to their families and were about to embark on their journey. One man's wife was upset, but he reminded her that he had put the uniform on long ago and they both knew what that meant, that they would have to sacrifice some things for the good of everyone. Two other men had gotten the call at six that morning and had rushed to Fort Eustis from their homes in the suburbs of Washington, D.C., where they served as apprentice firefighters. Both in their early twenties, they had spent the entire previous day fighting the fire at the Pentagon. One man had been on the roof and would never forget seeing American Airlines flight magazines scattered all over the place. Both had gone home exhausted, having been relieved after being on the scene for more than twelve hours.

The Port Security Unit arrived in lower Manhattan on Wednesday night and immediately set up the tent city they would live in for the entire time they were deployed. Their mission was "water-borne anti-terrorist force protection of major facilities." These included refineries, container facilities, and the USNS *Comfort*, a naval hospital ship used to house rescue workers. They had at their disposal six 25-foot tactical patrol boats with mounted .50 caliber machine guns and two mounted M-60 machine guns. Once their camp was established, they were on duty twenty-four hours a day, seven days a week.

This PSU was not the only Coast Guard Reserve unit called up. Hundreds of reservists from all over New York, New Jersey, and Connecticut had been called to duty the day before. And everyone, attorneys, teachers, plumbers, accountants, corporate executives, policemen, and firefighters, all showed up without delay and performed with honor and dedication.

At Ground Zero early Wednesday morning, a couple of dozen people in Coast Guard uniforms were observed moving around with some sort of hand-held monitors. "What in the world is the Coast Guard doing here?" one volunteer was heard to ask. It was the Atlantic Strike Force Team, the Coast Guard's quick response team from Fort Dix, New Jersey. They had driven up in an eighteen-wheel truck the day before at the request of the Environmental Protection Agency. The World Trade Center and surrounding area were now classified as a hazardous waste site. More than thirty toxic substances had emanated from the twin towers when they collapsed. Paints, chemicals, R-22 refrigerant, all kinds of dangerous materials were suddenly airborne. The Strike Force was providing preliminary air quality monitoring, work they normally would go about in full environmental suits. Not wanting to arouse public panic, however, they wore their normal uniforms and went about their work professionally and quietly, fully prepared to order an evacuation if they detected any life-threatening substances in lethal doses.

Also on Wednesday morning, activities in New York Harbor shifted from evacuation operations to coordinating vessel traffic for the delivery of emergency supplies and relief workers to Ground Zero. Lt. M.D. established three depots, at Battery Park, at Pier 32, and at North Cove. He authorized on-water fuel transfers for rescue boats so they did not have to leave the area and could continue working. He also authorized an order for 175,000 gallons of fuel without a purchase order or contract. Every vessel that arrived checked in with the Coast Guard and was assigned to a specific route based on size and maneuvering characteristics of the vessel.

At one point during the day, the volume of traffic became too high to manage by radio. So the lieutenant instructed all pilots to make visual contact with him on the *New York* located in the middle of the harbor. Then Lt. M.D. stood for hours on the bow of the pilot boat and directed rescue vessels like a traffic cop.

In the following days, weeks, and months, the United States Coast Guard maintained an active presence at Ground Zero and New York Harbor. At any given time, multiple teams of eight to ten Coast Guard firefighters were at Ground Zero aiding in relief efforts. "We train with the New York Fire Department all the time," said one. "We're searching for our friends."

At any given time, more than twenty members of the Coast Guard's Atlantic, Gulf, Pacific, and National Strike Force teams worked around the clock. They wrote up the safety plan for Ground Zero and for the Fresh Kills dumpsite. They conducted essential air checks in surrounding buildings. When equipment readings showed safe levels, technicians were allowed temporary access to their offices to remove hard drives and back-up computer systems. Strike Force team members also supervised washdown stations at the perimeter of the disaster site.

At any given time, eight Coast Guard chaplains could be found at Ground Zero. Twenty-nine of them rotated in and out to provide a listening ear, personal counseling, and various prayer and religious services. The chaplains also comforted the families of victims as they were transported across New York Harbor to the disaster site.

At any given time, members of the Coast Guard Auxiliary could be observed providing crisis counseling at a center they established a few blocks from Ground Zero. Private Auxiliary boats also transported media camera crews, relief supplies, New York firemen, policemen, and other rescue workers. And auxiliarists put themselves on the front lines with twenty-four-hour-a-day status, their boats fully manned. They covered search and rescue operations for the entire area while active duty personnel and reservists concentrated on port safety, security, waterways management, and homeland security.

The events of 11 September 2001 and its aftermath demonstrated the formidable leadership capabilities of the United States Coast Guard. Through resolute decisiveness, a strong bias for action, and effective communication, the organization was not only able to rush to the nation's rescue during the crisis, it was also able to shift gears and change the entire organization on a dime. And it did so, quite literally, overnight.

At 8:00 A.M. on that tragic day, less than 10 percent of the resources of the Coast Guard were allocated to port and homeland security. By the close of the next day, the percentage had risen to 57 percent. When the Commandant gave the order to "make a righthand turn and go to homeland security," not a soul or an asset in the Coast Guard stood idle.

Cutters on drug interdiction duty in the Caribbean made a beeline to major ports in the southeastern United States. Those in New England enforcing federal fishery laws took off to cover harbors in the Northeast. And it was the same for cutters on the West Coast, in Alaska, and in the South Pacific. Coast Guard law enforcement officers from Cleveland, New Orleans, and Portsmouth, Virginia, charged into New York City. All over the country, helicopters and planes, usually relegated to search and rescue operations, began flying reconnaissance along the nation's shorelines. Captains of the port immediately ramped up security at all the nation's ports, on the East and West Coasts, the Gulf of Mexico, the Great Lakes, Hawaii, Guam, and Puerto Rico. Small boat stations everywhere from Seattle to Miami, from San Diego to Boston, began twenty-four-hour security patrols. Coast Guard personnel boarded tankers, freighters, cruise ships, and other major vessels. They checked passenger manifests, inspected vessels for hazardous materials, and, when deemed necessary, provided armed escorts. And there were Coasties along every major inland river and waterway in the United States, the Mississippi, the Ohio, the Missouri, and the Potomac. You name it, the Coast Guard was there.

The organization's building of alliances and forging of relationships was also brought to bear in the crisis. The Navy did not hesitate to work with the Coast Guard in a joint effort to protect the nation's coastline, ports, and waterways. The New York Harbor Pilots Association helped willingly and without question in relief and port security actions. And all thirty-three thousand members of the Coast Guard Auxiliary poured out of their homes and offices to do whatever was asked of them, to assist, to fill in the gaps, even to take the lead in search and rescue operations. Because of their powerful alliance with the Auxiliary, the United States Coast Guard was able to double its forces overnight.

The concept of "team over self" and the principle of "leveraging resources" were also brought to the forefront. Team Coast Guard was able to coordinate efforts and work flawlessly with a variety of local, state, and federal agencies. Bureaucratic red tape and turf protection never entered the equation anywhere at any time. Everybody worked together to get the job done for the greater good. Coast Guard cutter crews willingly increased their terms of deployment. Personnel at small boat stations worked six and seven days a week, rotating twelve-hour shifts. Many labored around the clock until their supervisors had to order them to take time off. Nearly every active duty member of the Coast Guard was on twenty-four-hour standby for months. And members of the Coast Guard Reserve showed up by the thousands, manning Port Security Units, creating a new Sea Marshals program, and even later providing security at Guantanamo Bay, Cuba, where captured Al Qaeda and Taliban terrorists were held.

All around the Coast Guard, young people in the field were empowered to use their best judgment, make their own decisions, and take appropriate actions. And in every case, they rose to the occasion and performed with courage, excellence, and pride. In one of the most daunting crises in American history, the Coast Guard, along with New York's finest firefighters and policemen, were going into the disaster area when terrified victims were leaving. There were no spectators in the Coast Guard that day. On 11 September 2001, the United States Coast Guard exhibited leadership of the highest order and personified character in action.

———

Toward the end of September, the Commandant of the Coast Guard visited Ground Zero and took a helicopter tour of lower Manhattan. He was astonished to observe that Trinity Church, at the corner of Broadway and Wall Street (barely three blocks from the twin towers) had remained untouched through the devastation, even though nearly everything around it had suffered enormous damage.

Upon returning that evening to headquarters in Washington, D.C., the Commandant spoke with the Master Chief Petty Officer of the Coast Guard and told him about the church. "Vince, the graveyard has a foot of ash and debris all over it," he said. "Alexander Hamilton is buried there, along with many other American patriots."

"We'll take care of it, sir," came the response.

Vince quickly contacted the command master chief at Activities New York and explained the situation. The next day, a group of chiefs showed up at Trinity Church with the goal of cleaning the entire cemetery. Vince, who that morning had driven up from Washington to help in the effort, arrived to find the entire churchyard already cleaned, with several hundred bags of ash and dust stacked neatly to one side. The chiefs and the caretakers of Trinity Church had almost finished the entire job.

But the Master Chief Petty Officer of the Coast Guard saw one more thing that needed to be done. He grabbed a bucket of water, a washcloth, and a towel, went up to Alexander Hamilton's tombstone, and cleaned it until it sparkled. Then he and the other chiefs stood at attention and saluted the founding father of the Coast Guard.

Tuesday, 11 September 2001, was travel day for new recruits headed to Cape May, New Jersey. But the vast majority were stranded when the nation's air traffic system was shut down in the wake of the World Trade Center and Pentagon explosions. Some recruits were headed to the airport, some had already boarded planes, and some were actually in the air and ordered down.

Over the next four days, these young men and women straggled into Cape May from all over the country. They came by car, by bus, by train—some even hitchhiked. By Saturday, 15 September, one hundred percent of the new recruits had reported in. Eight weeks later, 135 young men and women graduated from the Training Center at Cape May and were sworn in as active duty members of the Coast Guard. The next day, they headed to their new stations, dedicated, committed, and determined to make a difference.

With its past preserved and its future ensured, the United States Coast Guard continues to serve the United States of America with Honor, Respect, and Devotion to Duty.

Index

About the Authors

Donald T. Phillips is a best-selling author of ten books. His most famous work is *Lincoln on Leadership*, which, through the history of the Civil War, elucidates Abraham Lincoln's leadership style and discusses how it can be used in today's complex society. *Lincoln on Leadership* is currently in its nineteenth printing and has been published in seven different languages. Phillips is also author of *The Founding Fathers on Leadership, Martin Luther King, Jr. on Leadership,* and *Leading With The Heart* and *Five-Point Play,* both coauthored with Mike Krzyzewski (Coach K of Duke University).

Phillips is a widely recognized figure in the field of leadership and historical scholarship. He has more than twenty-five years of experience in business and industry having held various managerial positions with several major corporations. He speaks frequently around the country to various business corporations, government groups, professional organizations, public schools, and institutions of higher learning.

Phillips has also held numerous private leadership positions and has served with distinction in local city government, including three terms as mayor of Fairview, Texas.

Admiral James M. Loy served as Commandant of the U.S. Coast Guard from May 1998 to May 2002. He graduated from the U.S. Coast Guard Academy in 1964 and holds master's degrees from Wesleyan University and the University of Rhode Island. He also attended the Industrial College of the Armed Forces and interned at the John F. Kennedy School of Government at Harvard University.

Admiral Loy has received two Department of Transportation Distinguished Service Medals, the Department of Defense Distinguished Service Medal, four Coast

Guard Distinguished Service Medals, the Bronze Star with Combat "V," the Combat Action Ribbon, and other military awards. He has been recognized by the American Society of Public Administration and Government Executive with their Leadership Award for 2001. He was named SEATRADE Personality of 2000 in London; he has also received the NAACP Meritorious Service Award for 2000 and was recognized by the Soldier's, Sailor's, Marine's and Airmen's Club with their Military Leadership Award for 2001. Admiral Loy has been inducted into the Reserve Officer Association's Minute Man Hall of Fame and received the U.S. Navy League prestigious Admiral Arleigh Burke Leadership Award for 2002.

Admiral Loy is currently the Administrator of the Transportation Security Administration. This agency was formed by the Aviation Transportation Security Act and is part of the newly formed Department of Homeland Security.